WISE
as #@%!

WISE
as #@%!

**Simple Truths
to Guide You Through
the $#!%storms of Life**

Gary John Bishop

HarperOne
An Imprint of HarperCollins*Publishers*

HarperOne

HarperCollins books may be purchased for educational, business, or sales promotional use. For information, please email the Special Markets Department at SPsales@harpercollins.com.

FIRST EDITION

Designed by Terry McGrath

Library of Congress Cataloging-in-Publication Data is available upon request.

ISBN 978-0-06-295227-1
ISBN 978-0-06-305203-1 (Merch. Ed.)
ISBN 978-0-06-305583-4 (Intl.)

20 21 22 23 24 LSC 10 9 8 7 6 5 4 3 2 1

I dedicate this book to anyone and everyone who wants more out of this life. No matter where you are or what you're doing, there is a way.

Contents

1

What to Do, What to Do . . .

Wisdom gets your shit together. It allows you to bring some fresh perspective and cuts a clear pathway through the morass of life.

Whatever your shitstorm is, at least one thing is clear. No one ever showed you how to handle this.

Where's the clarity or peace of mind or hell, just an inkling of what the fuck to do when life has crept up out of nowhere, kicked you right in the mouth, and now you're stopped dead in your tracks?

How are you supposed to sort through the mess or ease the anxiety or awaken the slumbering possibilities of your life while at the same time combating the daily press of your job situation, your relationships, your family, your body, your past, your future, and whatever else you want to throw in the mix like, oh, I don't know, some sort of global super-virus pandemic or something?

The truth is, we're painfully ill equipped for the storms and crashes that can happen to any of us.

It's not like we *want* to be flailing around in the chaos! No one aches to be anchored to the same cycle of a toxic relationship or a stifling career or to the painful reminders of love or failure or fear that we know all too well. We just want to move our lives forward, we want to know how to live our lives without the mysteries and confusions and complications. In short, we want help to make life better; we just don't know where to find this help, or how to make the right decision.

When life starts going wrong, of course it would be a lot easier if you could simply ask Alexa, plot your next genius move, and smoothly tiptoe into the future with your devastatingly smart use of Amazon products on standby for whatever comes next. Playlist, check, alarm, check, dictionary definition, check, how to handle your years-long burning resentments or dream-crippling procrastinations or need to make a life-altering decision on the fly . . . dammit, Alexa, show me some love!

Hey, maybe it's all in the diet, so perhaps I could interest you in a generous sprinkling of some tasty ancient, comforting wisdom on your avocado toast in the morning to help you navigate the day?

Yeah . . . no, not that either. It seems when we're most tested, we're least wise. The wisdom pantry is, unfortunately, mostly bare when you are starving for that all-knowing nutrient to help you powerfully take on whichever life-sucking situation is currently gnawing at the pit of your gut in any given moment.

Apparently you're supposed to make it up as you go along in the vain hope that one day you'll eventually stitch together some kind of useful life skills to manage your troubles and keep you in good order for what's to come. In the meantime, get your struggle on, Susan, and oh, yeah, keep that suffering silent, we're trying to be positive over here.

Yet we've all had those days.

Well, sometimes it's weeks.

Or months.

In some cases it has lasted so long it's hard to see anything else. The shitstorms of life can become so persistent they're just that. Life. The skies are gray and that's just how it is. Bring your brolly.

So we get on with it. None the wiser.

"None the wiser? But I AM wiser from my life experiences!!"

Not quite. If you think about it, "I'm never going to do that again" isn't really wisdom, is it? That can just be put down to good practice in life. My five-year-old has that down already and he's . . . well, he's five.

Nor is it a practice that applies to everything either. It's okay never to stick your hand onto a burning stove again, but the implications of never exposing yourself to love or opportunity or risk again can be devastating. You can become caged, trapped by your own doing. A dumbed-down, bored/scared out of your freaking mind version of yourself. Not so wise now, huh?

Simply put, you, like most people, take the completely wrong approach to both acquiring wisdom and then having it make a difference in the nitty-gritty of your life. Try on the idea you are looking for something to attach to your life, some insight or guidance or one-size-fits-all strategy that you can just plug in that will magically undo whatever shitshow you're currently starring in.

Let's set the record straight here.

That's not how wisdom works.

DEFINING WISDOM

I define wisdom as a personal set of truths, a collection of perspectives that become the foundations of your thinking and that you come back to throughout the twists and turns of your life to guide you. These truths not only give you clarity as you're making decisions, coming to crossroads, and trying to figure out which path to take, but they also make your next steps appear as obviously as your next breath.

Why do you need wisdom in your life? Well, first, if you're asking yourself that question and you've purchased a book called *Wise as Fu*k*, that's probably a bit of a clue!

But seriously, wisdom is something we all rely on from time to time, it's that all-knowing nugget of life that you either learned through lived experience or in a book or course or conversation.

I'll give you a simple example of the kind of wisdom I'm talking about and how it works right here: Have you ever heard the phrase "you have the life you're willing to put up with"?

Be with those words for a minute. As you let them sink in, think about and compare your own life to the statement and how you're currently living. What do you see there? At some point there will be something for you to consider or reconsider when you apply this wisdom to how you live.

There's a lot in those ten simple words, but they irretrievably put you in the spotlight, don't they? When you look at them it's hard to wriggle out of taking ownership of your life and how it's going. They bring to mind a view of life that demands you work your stuff out for yourself, to tolerate or procrastinate no longer. They root you to a truth—if you're willing to adopt them as your own, that is. This uncomplicated statement deals with any temptation for blame or gossip or victimizing oneself or others. Try it out if you're ever faced with a situation where you want to blame someone for what's going wrong. I dare you to turn to this statement. Here's what will happen. It will tell you what to do.

And that's how wisdom works, by this process of first understanding, adopting as your own, and then applying to your real life. Keep this critical process in mind as we navigate these pages together. You are your own hero, but you could just as easily turn yourself into the one who constantly needs to be rescued. Good wisdom will end those days. It puts you back in charge of your life, your future. You get to create the life you want. No one else can take that from you. Isn't that empowering?

If wisdom comes from a set of internal, guiding truths, how do you determine *what* those truths are for you?

Let's broach this process of thinking first. Have you ever "pondered" something? I don't mean just a fleeting thought, or just a brief reflection. Have you ever sat with an idea or a question long enough to open it up for yourself in new ways such that you taught *yourself* something? Your own personal aha. A proper discovery.

That's the beginning of where the wisdom in this book will take root in your life. From your own inquiry, the kind of introspection and retrospection that enlivens and enlightens, inspires and invigorates an otherwise stodgy and numb existence. The cool thing is, real wisdom can never be undone, because when you discover something for yourself, such as a thunderous, penetrating discovery, you cannot undiscover that thing. But it doesn't stop with the discovery. You take it on by consciously adopting it, then plow straight into your life and live from it. That's what makes it so distinct from knowledge. Just about anyone can read something, maybe even memorize it too, but not everyone is learning from it and then living from what they've learned.

It does, however, take some work to think deeply and discover the truths at the center of your life. It's easier, it seems, to look for a "how to" strategy instead. The problem is, that doesn't work because it only scratches the surface of your life. We want instant answers without diving into what's at the bottom, to a place where lives a boundless wisdom that could provide you with far more than turn-and-burn solutions to irritating, passing problems. That's why your "five steps to success" strategies just fall apart at some point, because you are never at the source of them. Everyone wants a simple answer; everyone wants to be told how to *do* success or dieting or love, because at some level they just don't want to think beyond the limits of their own confusion or apathy or the story they've created about themselves.

Most people also believe that to experience lasting personal transformation, you need to hear or read something brand-new. Not the case. It all comes down to you and whether you're engaging with the material to shift something meaningful, or just vacuuming data to momentarily get yourself off.

Often, when we think of someone being "wise," what we mean is "they know a lot of stuff" or that they possess some admirable character trait such as patience or compassion or whichever virtuous trait that seemingly comes so easily to them. But just because someone has memorized the entire dictionary doesn't make them wise, does it? Is knowing how to define "cataclysmic" going to help them out when their life goes up in flames and they need to find a way to douse the fire? Not so much.

Over time, you can forget facts and figures. Things get lost in the fog of our complicated lives and wispy memories. Even the things you do remember don't always make a difference. They fall out your mouth like the score from last night's Yankees game or Grandma's favorite cookie recipe. Accurate but nonetheless toothless in the fight for peace of mind or clarity or power.

Some of the most knowledgeable people I've met could hardly be described as wise.

And vice versa, of course.

In any case, all the new knowledge in the world will never change the machine until the machine finally examines itself. And when I say machine, of course, I mean you.

In this book about wisdom, I'm talking about the kind of learning that genuinely changes *you*. Makes you wiser. Presents opportunities for growth. You see, the things that I have authentically discovered in my life changed me. Forever. There was no going back from it. When you realize it's been you all along, it sticks in your throat when you try to blame someone else. You can smell your own bullshit from quite a distance after a while, too.

I live my life totally, wholly, and completely from the streetwise principles set forth here. These are the guidelines I apply to my life, and I don't fuck with them. They are robust and non-negotiable, and they have never let me down. Does that make me perfect, floating on a thin bed of existential magic goo, constantly in touch with greatness and all things wonderful in this life? NO! I'm a human being. Just like you I get challenged and stopped and pissed off and stuck in random swamps of bullshit and confusion, but do you know what? My fucking life WORKS!! I have simple answers available to me every day of my life, and there's no reason why you can't have them too.

Someone once told me, "if you want to be successful, do what successful people do," and that notion applies to absolutely everything, but it fits both sides of the coin.

If you're currently miserable, you're probably doing what miserable people do. However, if you want to be rich, you'll need to do what rich people do, if you want to be fit, do what fit people do, AND if you want to be wise and have a life that works . . . well, you get the picture.

You and I are going to turn your fucking life around here. You bring your time and the most attention your eager noggin can muster, and let's make sparks fly.

WHAT WE'RE IN FOR HERE

Before we get in too deep, we're going to figure out what truths guide you. To work that part out, it's critically important to distinguish good wisdom from bad wisdom. We'll spend the next part of this book learning how to tell them apart. And it's trickier than you might think. By the time we've brought good and bad wisdom to light we'll be ready to get into some fundamentals of life. You know, the most basic of stuff—such as love and the lack of it—that seems to derail all your best plans and leave you high and dry. We'll put some real and lasting wisdom at your fingertips to handle those fundamentals now and in the future. We'll talk more about those in the next chapter.

A few words of wisdom (get it?) before you get started.

First, TAKE YOUR TIME. There's a lot of stuff here that will go unnoticed if you read this in a sloppy or haphazard way. Do not hurry to finish or you'll miss the whole point. Pause, breathe, think, break these words down for yourself. If you don't understand something, that's a good time to stop and do some genuine thinking. Don't move on from any part of this book until it resonates with you. Becoming wiser begins by taking a wise approach.

You can't just instantly stir yourself up the kind of wisdom you're going to use for the rest of your days like a quick cup of Starbucks VIA. Slow down, think, percolate, let these words rise in your life.

You have to completely immerse yourself in the truth first and then deal with your entire life from it and yes, that's right, your entire life, not just the bits that are a little fucked right now.

It's a process of continually looking at the wisdom you've discovered and asking yourself, "Given this truth, which parts of my life are out of sync with it, and what do I now need to do to have them line up?"

Doing so might first throw up a series of problems; no-kidding, real-life concerns that will demand you do something about certain areas of your life that you've been ignoring, neglecting, or in denial about.

In the moments of comparing your life with the words in this book, your emotions might squirm and kick back, but remember you are out to be guided by something other than the roller coaster of your predictable feelings, thoughts, or circumstances, right? To live a powerful life you need something that lives outside of your everyday responses, a voice that's independent, reliable, and brings you back to a settled place. Wisdom.

Real, lasting wisdom rises in your moments of need; it separates you from the pack, moves you in new directions, and lives on and on in the very fabric of your being. It adds depth and meaning and quality to our lives. You don't just *know* that thing you learned, you *are* that thing now, and you won't need the Instagram fantasy of a Bugatti or blingy new watch to Band-Aid your insecurities anymore either.

You won't think like everyone else and you won't get weighed down by the usual mundane shit that most people do because you have a loaded toolbox, ready at hand and ready to go. And you can build a life around that shit too.

Also, when we get into the fundamentals, I encourage you to genuinely ponder what I'm saying. What does it take to ponder something? Well, it's kinda like "hanging out" with an idea. No formed opinion, no need to define or come to some decision, just an opportunity for you to let an idea ferment in your mind. You sit with it, you revisit it and let it speak to you. You consider the words and what they mean or don't mean. Then you question that too.

You might recollect situations from your past and compare them to what's being said, or you might use your current situation to deepen what you are reading here. In any case, make this real for yourself; your life isn't a fucking concept, so stop engaging with it like it is.

This is about making you wiser, remember?

DON'T QUOTE ME

It would be remiss of me to ignore an important point here. The wiser I become, the weirder I sound to some people. It's not a problem; I'm far more likely to nod my head these days than to take someone to task over their particular views on life.

Let me explain with an example.

If you follow me online, particularly on Instagram (@garyjohnbishop), you'll already know that I'm fond of the odd quote or seventy. Almost every day I'll put something out there that's designed to stimulate the brain, to get you to interrupt your own meanderings of life; but often, almost as soon as the thing is posted . . . mayhem.

People disagree, people get pissed off and sanctimonious, others get confused with a healthy dose of WTF. Some ask for an explanation or, at the very least, straighten me out with how I *should* have said it so that it doesn't seem so offensive or cold or frivolous or . . . well, you get the picture.

The thing is, these are from people who *follow* me!

Why is that? Partly because of my style of writing, which is generally confrontational. It can hit a nerve, sometimes to the point of pain. I prefer to say things that you cannot escape from, the kind of stuff that boxes you in and forces you to think. I'm never out to write things that make you feel better. I'm out to produce the kind of stuff that does violence to your apathy and resignation.

But that's only a tiny part of why people respond in the ways they do.

Most importantly, this comes down to the mode in which people engage with what they read, which is in a simplistic, observational one of comparison. You're basically scanning the world looking for stuff to agree or disagree with. Not you? Yes, you too. Your disagreement with my point is exactly what I'm talking about here. Try on the idea you're looking for the familiar, something that resonates with what you already think, know, or believe.

Then in a blink of time, you instantly start to compare. You might not realize that's what you're doing, but the urge to agree or disagree is something that resides in all of us like an insatiable hunger. It's why politics is such a furious beast. And family's fracture. And love gets destroyed. It's not new, either; it's very human, but like a lot of human stuff, it doesn't always work. That voracious appetite for agreeing or disagreeing has ruined many a friendship, partnership, or love, particularly when followed by the impenetrable brick wall of "who's right." This isn't a concept that's new to you either, is it?

When we hear or read something, if it fits, we like it, if it doesn't, we might ignore it, but if it fiercely collides with some deeply rooted truth or belief, the urge to voice our disapproval can take over. When it all comes down to it, this is about survival. The survival of your own comforting little mirage of reality and safety.

I might be saying something that would require you to take stock of some things you've done in your life or justified about yourself, something you'd built excuses around that, when challenged, might put you in a bit of a spot and not a particularly comfortable one either. You might need to deal with a harsh truth you had never considered or had perhaps even willfully ignored. It's not just others who might get a little fucked up by your sparkly new transformation. You most likely will too.

Like a lot of what I write, be prepared for that experience arising in the turn of any given page here.

No wonder new stuff can bend us so spectacularly out of shape. It becomes a threat. As I said earlier, as your wisdom grows, you might become a threat to someone's else's mirage. It's okay. Be responsible, be compassionate, and let that shit go. Everyone has to grow in their own way and in their own time, and just because you're not at the same spot as someone else doesn't make you better or farther along or in any way superior. It's not a race or pyramid of enlightenment.

You are at where you are at; they are at where they are at. End of story. Sometimes it just takes a while for people to come to terms with your new realization or epiphany or growing sense of yourself. Breathe. They'll get there, just as you did. If they don't, you'll be so enlightened you won't give a damn anyway.

Everybody wins!

A WISE AS FU*K LIFE

Finally, we'll discuss what a truly Wise as Fu*k life looks like. Living wisely is definitely about navigating our daily, weekly, and monthly circumstances and, yes, struggles. But without spoiling anything, it looks a lot bigger than you could even imagine. It's the kind of life where you and what you stand for matter in this world. A big fucking life.

Wisdom eventually makes sense of the mess, but at the same time it will demand that you clean up that very same mess. And that, my friend, is often a messy process in itself!

However, be left in no doubt that wisdom tells you the truth. What you do with that truth could be the single biggest turning point of your life.

Or not. If you want this book to be different, you'll need to be different too, at least in how you read and engage with it. By the end of this book you'll have yourself some real wisdom. Something you can build on and learn from and grow the tree of this life of yours in a direction of your own magnificent creation rather than just a series of boring reactions to seemingly uncontrollable outside influences, random feelings, or freaks of fate.

Wisdom gets your shit together. It allows you to bring some fresh perspective and cuts a clear pathway through the morass of life.

A peace of mind to reach for when you get dumped or you fail or your best friend dies, the kind of stuff that we want to ignore but that can and, most likely, will happen. When someone tells you that you can't do it and somewhere deep inside you agree with them, when those feelings of shame or panic or guilt shut you down or you're gripped by the all-consuming fear of the unknown. Then there's the choking sea of procrastinations, "I'm gonnas" and "if onlys" that can slow a life to a throat-jarring stop.

The show must go on, ready or not.

Because whether you realize it or not, we're out for a life that matters. Your life is too important to let that pass by! You are a fucking miracle of being, remember?

Got that curiosity itch yet? Great! Let's get scratching!

2

Bad Wisdom

Never allow yourself to settle for "feeling better" about a life that doesn't work. That's called stagnation and, as clichéd as it might sound, you actually are better than that.

Turns out there's a lot of really bad wisdom out there. Stuff that's easy to consume, and on the surface it makes sense but isn't as helpful as it might seem. We hear these cliché phrases from our friends when they're trying to make us feel better, we read them on greeting cards and inspirational posters, and they're all over social media. Picture those memes that explain your mess in about a dozen words, sometimes poetically or romantically. While it may make you feel good for a moment, rather than igniting a fire or launching you toward personal transformation, it actually sinks you a little deeper into the shit you're already in. Stuff like:

"What's for you will come to you." No, it fucking won't. You're not a train station. Do something!

"Believe in yourself." What if you don't; are all bets off? Jeez. Just get into action, will you?

"Surround yourself with positive people." Yeah . . . but what if those "positive people" think *you're* the asshole and want no part of your bs? Oh, I get it, hang around anyway and suck the positivity out of them, and when you're done, find yourself a new group to bleed dry, right?

"You become what you think about." So close . . . but no. If you don't act on those thoughts, you won't become your thoughts at all. Also, I think about puppies quite a bit and still no sight of a tail.

"Happy thoughts, happy life." Hmm . . . maybe, but what if I'm depressed or someone close to me has died or I just got fired or my house just got robbed? Oh, well, I guess I should just cheer up then. Fucking yay.

You might be thinking, Well, so what? If it makes me feel better, isn't that the point?

No.

Most online material is designed to give you momentary relief, to make you feel better about your mess without waking you up to a change. Often it just allows you to confirm you were right, even when there's that nagging doubt you may not have been. Feeling better just isn't enough. You can never allow yourself to settle for feeling better about a life that doesn't work. That's called stagnation and, as clichéd as it might sound, you actually are better than that.

We're here to make real, lasting change with our lives, and that's why it's so important to dig down into some real wisdom to consistently guide your decisions and actions.

When we get to the chapters about love and loss and success and failure, I'm going to give you some new phrases, words with real depth and a powerful meaning to replace these shallow and gutless "bad wisdom" phrases. The difference between them and this? Interruption. I'm out to make you think, to question, and to challenge the norms of your life.

If you read *Unfu*k Yourself*, you'll remember we did this there too. We interrupted the repetitive scripts that run through our heads and invented a new kind of truth. A new wisdom, if you like.

Bad wisdom can come from well-intentioned places too. You might be wondering, what about the advice we get from our friends or family? "Do this" or "do that" isn't wisdom. That's advice. Advice is what we seek when we're out of ideas or any real thinking to work our shit out on our own, so we'll ask someone else to tell us what to do. At least if it goes to hell, we can always blame them, right?

Enlightenment rule no. 10087: Stop asking people what you should do; engage your own brain, read, discover, and plot your path.

For what it's worth, your hunger for advice is really about your desire to tell others about your predicament, how you've handled it, and to get their agreement that you're doing the "right thing." You're not really looking for advice at all. You're mostly looking for the friendly seal of approval.

Okay, pause. I can hear the "yeah, but" bubbling in your mind. Here's some advice right here: you'll have to catch and drop that driving addiction to "yeah, but" if there's any chance of this book waking you up to something new. I find that people usually insert their own "yeah, but" into these kinds of books just so they don't have to address the discomfort of the point being made. A single, solitary objection is often enough for them to dismiss the entire opportunity for growth. I'm here to help you grow. So try to be patient and stick with me as we uncover the places where that needs to happen in your life.

There are also people with good intentions (for the most part) dishing out bad wisdom to either get paid or get likes or approval or avoid their own shit and as long as it's displayed in a natty font with a misty picture of a waterfall or the fucking sunset or swished down with a cup of five-dollar java, we're good to go!

Unfortunately, this can also stretch into the world of self-help (ugh), with an ocean of books, mastermind groups, workshops, courses, journals, planners, and summits absolutely brimming with bad wisdom, strategically seducing people with the presentation of the material rather than making a real difference for the reader or participant. Well-intentioned bad wisdom is still bad wisdom.

Yes, I'm fully aware that I write books that are typically found in the self-help section of the bookstore. But what sets this apart is we're not just putting a metaphysical Band-Aid on your issues. Rather, we're getting real with how you live your life and what it looks like to start building something new. A new life based on a solid foundation of principles and ideas. Wisdom.

THE ART OF THINKING

As I was writing this book, it was quite the problem for me to work out how to give *you* something that, if you dwelled on it long enough, you could turn into lifelong wisdom, the kind of insight available to you for the rest of your life just when you needed it most. A fresh perspective, a completely new view.

A way of seeing things that if you finally saw it, there would be no way to unsee it. No going back. A wisdom that changes not only how you see life but also how you interact with it. And when you interact with this new understanding, these truths, it could actually change your life. It could fix your broken relationship with your mother, could smooth over the tensions at work, could unleash you to write that book already!

It's actually not that hard to reframe how you see failure or fear or love or success. That part begins in your mind. The real challenge begins when you step out there into the cold, hard surface of your life and start to approach your relationships or your career or your passions from a brand-new perspective. When you no longer deal with these things in a way that you've wired yourself to, it may well seem like an alien landscape, where you're not so nimble or sure of yourself, particularly to begin with.

Nothing looks the same when you're looking at your life from a different view.

The reason you keep running into the same problems in life is because you are always engaging with them from the same angle. You have become so obsessed with trying to fix the problems from this particular view, you have forgotten your ninja power—you can shift your angle on it. You can stand in a new place and look out and handle life from there.

Imagine this. You are standing on top of a hill and looking into a valley, and in the distance, there is a small town. You want to get to that town. From where you are standing you start to think of that river you need to get across or the thick, muddy field to traverse, or that dense, dark woods you'll have to hack your way through, combined with an endless series of obstacles, detours, and conditions that you can both see and imagine.

You're building a picture in your mind and plotting your solution. You might be recollecting other times when you've walked or run or that piece of advice you heard from your dad or read in a book.

Wow . . . this is going to be tough.

Add what you know about yourself and your mind-set, your strength, what you already think you can and can't do, what you're wearing or don't have with you, you might be thirsty or hungry or just having an "off" day and you're now starting to get a real sense of what this is going to take to get there.

You might even be reconsidering whether you could or even should do this at all. What's the point? It's just some dumb town, anyway. That's the problem with towns; they're always hard to get to. They're more bother than they're worth . . . right?

Now, you and I both know that conclusion is absurd.

But try on the idea that that's exactly how you live your life. You keep looking at the same shit from the same standpoint, somehow hoping that it will eventually get better while occasionally plugging in someone else's random advice and bad wisdom, going nowhere, ever hopeful. Here's the deal. If you keep standing where you're standing, you will continue to see the same view with the same ideas, solutions, problems, and obstacles. It's never what you're up against but rather where you are seeing it from that has you in this pattern.

Now, you might not like the view you have but you've also become a little comfy with it, you've eked out an existence, made some friends, cobbled together a life, made this shit work up on that little hill of yours. And you'll die with this perspective. It will become everything, and you'll never see it unless you challenge it, which is exactly what I'm tasking you with. Challenging your own view of how things are or should be. Taking an existential sledgehammer to some of your "sacred cows" and testing yourself in the uncertainty and unease of a different perspective. One that you might either never have heard of or had previously dismissed because it's there, right in the middle of that new view of yours that you could build a new view of your life, one that opens doorways and pathways and routes you had never even seen or considered.

We're now in the kind of place where we can begin addressing those fundamentals I talked about earlier. Keep your mind open and your commitment to change close by. You might well need them the deeper we go.

FUNDAMENTALS OF LIFE

What I love about this book is that it gives me the opportunity to touch on subjects I typically don't get to in my books. It's so easy to focus our energy on pursuing things such as motivation, money, houses, and "stuff," and it's a lot harder (and to be honest, less enjoyable) to invest ourselves in being powerful with the things that derail us. Tragedy, misfortune, theft, scandal, or trouble of one kind or another can touch anyone's life. Wouldn't you want to not only be prepared for that, but also equipped to rebuild your life in its aftermath?

I don't know about you, but hope isn't a risk I'm willing to take. Ever.

That's why I've split this book up into sections that I call "fundamentals of life." Y'know, the cornerstones of what we all have to face, stuff such as the rudderless experience of **loss** or the complexities of **love** or the nervous and energy-draining minefields of **success** and **failure**. By working through these four categories, it will allow you some space to get your arms around what's going on with you and your situation. The topics are wide, but the wisdom is both profound and useful.

Some people think to compartmentalize their life to try to make sense of it. To separate this thing from that thing. Work life from private life, or family life from social life.

It's all bullshit. It's always you, regardless of the compartment. I've lost count of the number of times I've interacted with people who proclaim, "my life is fine except [insert compartment here]" and then go on to explain some character flaw or sucky family life or career or trail of broken relationships/friendships or business ventures and if they could only fix this one thing, they'd be amazing. STOP!! Your "life" is not fine; stop fooling yourself and lowering the fucking bar!

The reality is, you can't turn off being yourself from one situation to the next. You're only ever freer to be your fullest, most authentic self in one place when compared to another, but it's *always* you. It's never not you. Where you are freest, you are happiest. Where you are constrained, you are most disempowered, but even if it's only with one item in your life, that kind of personal suppression bleeds into everything, and I mean *everything*, whether you realize it or not. Don't kid or buy yourself off with this notion of "everything but . . ." It's all or nothing, and you can have it all working in your favor with enough wisdom to handle life when it occasionally does go in the wrong direction.

You might start seeing problems with the constraining areas of your life here and the complete unworkability of how you have sheepishly accepted them as "just how it is." Fuck that. You *can* have it all, and you should accept nothing less. Period.

In each fundamental chapter, I'll share a handful of phrases I use that will then become the *beginnings* of a pathway for you to explore on your own. I'll give you a little tip here. Don't skim through the pages. Let yourself sit with the words, take notes if you want, maybe even highlight or underline the parts you want to dive into in the comfort of your own questions and thinking. Take your time, but most of all, allow yourself the discomfort of the challenge.

Remember, the temptation to agree or disagree with these phrases will most definitely crop up. You'll have to continually set that aside so that you can hang with the idea long enough to join the dots. You might have a lot of real-life situations that fiercely conflict with what I'm proposing. Try on the idea that it's not the situations of your life that conflict with what I'm saying here but rather the current "wisdom" you have used to get yourself into those situations. If you've lived your entire life believing that love is this way or that, it's going to be confronting when I say something that feels like the complete opposite to what you've built your life on. I'm challenging you to sit with that tension—that's where change happens, and that's the good stuff!

The life you have is a product of the views and ideas that you currently believe to be "true," but when you look at that same life using different principles, you'll see a clash. That's okay. In fact, it's exactly what we want to see.

Some of these phrases you might be familiar with; some you might think you "already know," but do not be fooled. This is an opportunity to go beyond "knowing" into the world of wisdom and insight. On many occasions in my life I have reexamined things I thought I knew and eventually learned something completely different. As life moves to new areas, it's important to reexamine seemingly old ideas for new wisdom from the perspective of where your life is now.

The creeping arrogance of already knowing can catch even the smartest of human beings, although perhaps not so much as the automatic surrender and numbness of apathy. A while ago I posted a meme on social media along the lines of "one of these days you will die." A few people responded with a dull ambivalence about the quote, and one person dismissed the quote as old news.

Your life will end is *old news*?!! I mean, how fucking jaded are you??!!!

I have never taken the idea that I'm going to die with anything other than the seriousness it deserves. That I will one day die wakes me up to life. Every. Single. Day. If you've become blasé about the inevitability of your own departure from this life . . . wake up. You're asleep at the wheel. You can engage with the material here like a workbook or a reference guide or, in times of distress, a source of insight and clarity to put some solid ground under your feet. A wisdom you can count on. Keep this book near. Keep it in your purse or on your desk or in your kitchen or by your bed, anywhere you can get to it regularly and in times of great need. It won't let you down. Don't just read. Study, drink it down, and let yourself be informed and expanded. Your own wisdom will arise from the thoughts between passages.

This is your shot to truly develop yourself, to thicken your skin and widen your outlook. To become someone who can navigate life powerfully and reliably. I should add a smidgen of bad news right about now. As with all my work, you might uncover stuff here that will require you to reexamine your current life. It might also demand some significant and difficult life change from you. Do not falter. Do not hide. Lean in. You got this.

Keep in mind, everything I do is designed for you to change your life. I also make it my business to have this material be at a price most people can afford. The days of real personal development applying only to those who can afford tens of thousands of dollars are over as far as I'm concerned. If you apply what I'm saying here, you will change your life. But if you're a self-help junkie with little or no results to show for all your "efforts," consider that you are all out of excuses now. Don't add this book to the "read but didn't do anything with" pile on the shelf.

The trick in this book is to slowly settle your life into the various passages, to soak up the ideas, think in the spaces between the lines, wrestle with the elements, and listen to yourself. Connect your situation, your problems and dramas, steep in these words, and listen to what begins to arise. You might well surprise yourself with your innate ability to think great things and make them happen.

So with that in mind, let's tackle our first fundamental of life.

Love.

This is such a heavyweight topic of opinion; position; and, at times, mystery but it's certainly one where we could all do with at least a bit of wisdom from time to time, right?

Okay . . . in we go.

3

Love

*Lasting, powerful love
is consciously choosing
to love another for
ALL that they are,
not just the good bits
that we approve of or
find most agreeable.*

Holy shit, how do you even tackle this thing?

Love is such a monumental part of our humanity that at first glance it seems like a complicated mess of chest-bursting aliveness, ego, trust/mistrust, despair, worry, elation, gut-churning excitement, bone-exposing vulnerability, sometimes anger, profoundly deep human connection, and whichever random roller coaster of emotion you care to throw in the mix for good measure.

Some people have a blissful, love-conquers-all attitude to the subject, while others have become so resigned to the notion of love that they're dead to the very idea. You might be either one of these people or maybe you're somewhere in the middle—one foot in, one foot out.

Some meaningful wisdom here and there could make all the difference in this potpourri of drama, wants, and strategy. For such a pivotal, important part of our lives, why is it so intangible, so out of reach at times?

Love is one of those fundamentals of life that both delights and frustrates, enlivens and destroys in one way or another. But it's also a subject of a fairly even smattering of disagreement and hocus-pocus. As an example, we've all heard of "love at first sight." It's both a common expression and a regular source of debate.

The more romantic among us insist that there is such a thing, that we can know the "one" simply by seeing them or hearing their voice. From the moment we connect with that special angel from afar, our heart is sent soaring and our mind reeling. A beam of light pierces the clouds and a flock of doves is released as your soul mate appears through a haze of misty, magical love gas and walks into your open arms, universes collide, and the stars align. Then, hand in hand, you both effortlessly hop into the love basket, dangling majestically below the giant ecstasy balloon, and off you float into the stratosphere for all eternity.

Or something.

Then suddenly, one dark day, you catastrophically fall out of the love basket, hurtle toward Earth at the mind-bending speed of holy shit and BAM!

It's over.

Damn, so that's what they mean when they say they "fell out of love." No wonder it's so agonizing!

Should've gotten yourself a love seat belt or at the very least a love parachute (or is that what the affair was all about?).

Others, the more cynical, find this all positively silly. They argue that there's absolutely no such thing as love at first sight and don't even start with that basket and parachute nonsense either.

Believe it or not, there are those who even question whether love, at least as *we* conceive of the notion, exists at all. That it's little more than a function of neurons connecting and the body responding while we eagerly follow the trail like lost wanderers seduced by the possibility of a new horizon.

Let's be honest here, though: I think we can all agree that it doesn't sound very romantic to say, "Hey, the old neurons are firing in sequence here, so we should probably get married" . . . right?!

LOVE IN THE REAL WORLD

For most of us, our notion of love lives in the misty vapors of our thoughts, whether our version is the logical version or the romantic version or somewhere in the chasm between. It's an amalgamation of pictures and memories of events, learned ideals, and all intertwined with certain habitual emotions and behaviors.

Hardly a recipe for clarity and real power in this arena, is it?

Whether it's romantic love or familial love, the love of a friend or animal or your authentic love for all people or certain situations, when I talk about love here, I mean the kind of love that applies to all of it. In short, I'm talking about you and the way you deal with love in your real life. How you express yourself, suppress yourself, use love to dominate by trying to guilt others, or desperately churn your way through people as you search for "the one" who will be the answer to your terminally unanswerable question.

Here I want you to look at the ways you love in your life. Not anyone else's behaviors or love as some sort of concept. I'm talking about your current situation and love you share with your friends (or not), how you love your mom or your partner or your cat or your kid. Obviously I'm including the idea that there are those you don't express your love for or find yourself too caught up in resentment or hate for you to even consider love as an option.

LOVE AS A CHOICE

Part of the problem with loving another is that it generally includes a surge of reality-bending dopamine in your brain that tends to mask a lot of things that, in the case of romantic love, only start to get revealed once you're knee deep in them. What used to delight you about that person or situation can eventually become what you're driving yourself nuts with too! *Sayonara* dopamine, hello resignation, doubt, and the subtle hues of resentment liberally splattered across your daily conversations.

When that inevitably happens, we can all too easily start to get soured and begin picking things apart. Of course, like everything, it begins in your head. A doubt here, a question there when things start to take a turn down. It builds in layers over time. In many ways, all our love relationships are prone to this process, even the love we have for our parents or friends or our children. True, authentic love isn't just about appreciating the best parts of a person. Anyone with an ounce of compassion or decency can appreciate someone's physical beauty or character or intelligence. That shit's easy.

Lasting, powerful love, however, is consciously choosing to love another for ALL that they are, not just the good bits that we approve of or find most agreeable. Particularly when you're tested to go another route. To disconnect or betray. I should point out that betraying someone isn't just confined to having an affair. You can betray another by bailing out on who you were when you came into this thing.

You might be physically still in it, but that's about it.

If you dig a little deeper, you'll eventually see you're not betraying that person, you're betraying who you said you are or would be. It's one of those betrayals of self. But what makes it worse isn't even the betrayal, it's the pretending that you're not doing that, that does the damage. You see, no matter the reasons and justifications you might have for doing what you do, you are the one continuing with this sham, and while it can be handy every now and again to have a scapegoat for all your bullshit, surely this is a step too far?

Tick-tock, the clock is ticking, and your sham life is passing you by.

Therefore, to truly love someone, in other words, is to love the whole, to choose to love their entire person and personality, for better or for worse.

Love is, by its very nature, unconditional. And when I say unconditional, I really mean it has no options but love itself. It flows, it's irresistible, and it's all-consuming. Unconditional love is the only kind of love that exists. I know people use the term "love with conditions," but that's some other phenomenon. It's like something is now getting in the way of that fully expressed love you are. It's hesitant, measured, judged, sometimes painfully so. That isn't love. That's a strategy for surviving something. I can hear your disagreement from here . . . cut it out.

Love doesn't hurt, by the way. Love is fucking awesome. Disappointment is what *hurts*, and your expectations are the vehicle that will drive you inch by inch into that hole.

You're not upset at the love in your life, you're upset at the absence of the love you thought you'd have, and when you find yourself there, you'll see that you are actually outside of your situation, you are observing it and judging it. You are no longer in it in the ways that you once were. You are no longer on the hook for the love in your life. The burden for that lies with someone else, and they are who you are now observing.

Now, on the other hand, when you do love someone all the way to the pudgy tips of your cute little doughy toes, conditions are the last thing on your mind.

Let's be clear here, though. I'm not saying that you must continue to love someone, no matter the circumstances, and live in complete denial of all they may do or say.

There are definitely occasions that when two people come together, the results are more harmful than healthy. And if you find yourself in a situation like this, I'm not saying that you must continue loving this person for all eternity.

Love exists in a moment of time. The present. Love is always in the present. When it's there, when you are in the presence of love, while it's unmistakable and unconditional, it doesn't mean it's unconditional everything else too. I can love you and disagree with you but only until my disagreement starts to spoil that connection. That's when the self-righteousness or resentment or anger or frustration takes over the house and keeps the imaginary suitcase handy . . . just in case.

People will spend years fantasizing their "escape" while completely standing still. Worse still, many are in their current relationship already plotting what they'll do differently in the next one, like this is a trial run for their Hallmark fantasy.

There could come a point in your future, whether ten years from now or ten days, when you just can't tolerate someone else's "stuff." When you find yourself no longer willing to choose that person—maybe you're even hating them now. Perhaps they cheated, stole from you, or have indulged their own demons for just too long. Their life could be trailing off in a direction you hadn't planned for nor agreed to.

Whatever has gotten in the way might now be something you are opposed to tackling any longer.

Your job, in those times, is to take ownership of *your* unwillingness. No blame, no bs drama, it's over, and you're taking a stand for something new. If you are to leave a relationship, leave with the kind of care and honor you went into it with, regardless of how the other person is responding to this situation. It's called personal integrity. Abuse it at your peril.

"Yeah, but . . ." Deal with yourself.

(Note to self—definitely write a kick-ass book about relationships.)

However, at this moment in time, the people you truly love are the people you love wholly, both the good and the bad. A whole and complete love.

FOR THE LOVE OF A HUMAN

To love is to suffer and there can be no love otherwise.
—Fyodor Dostoevsky

At first read, this quote by Dostoevsky may seem a little harsh, but it makes total sense when you realize the importance that he placed on love. Love is critical, it is essential to our nature—but that doesn't mean it's a fairy tale. There is a good and a bad to any loving relationship, whether it's with your spouse, your parents, or your weird Aunt May.

Why is love so crucial? Because human beings are essentially nothing but love. It is who we are. All of us.

"Huh???!!!"

Yes. All of us.

Now, your mind may already have jumped to some particularly nasty people you know or have recently encountered. If human beings are love, then why is your landlord such a grumpy old toad? Right?

Why is your dad so cynical or your sister so spiteful? Why is your boss SUCH an ass? I mean, come on, people are mostly love, but there are some real jackasses in your life, especially your ex. Right?

But I assure you it's true, though it's a lot more obvious when we're born. Little ones can express love in the most surprising of circumstances at times. And there's nothing in the way. Nothing.

But as we age and grow, different elements of our lives and our surroundings begin to block that love, so that we have trouble expressing it with being as loving, as we could otherwise.

What about "evil" people? Well, first, that's a violently overused word that I've heard applied dramatically to situations where it just doesn't belong. In most cases, not only does it not apply, it also makes the situation much, much worse than it needs to be. Second, a better perspective is that while we all begin on the same pathway, we do not all follow it in the same way. Some human beings become derailed; their thoughts, emotions, and behaviors take them in an initially unhealthy direction and eventually toward a very dark and destructive one. In any case, we're talking about an overall tiny part of the world's population who might behave in such a manner, so let's get back to the shitstorms of you and your life.

You see, we can all too easily become soured and defensive and strategic about love in all its forms. Being in a bad mood, dominating the situations of your life, being righteous and positioned about who is right and who is wrong. Withholding and using your love as a weapon to have this situation turn out the way you want it to. Domination, domination,

domination. That's right, even when you feel as if you're the injured party too.

There are the long-forgotten decisions you made as a teenager or as a young adult when you were humiliated or violated or rejected. While the memory lives on, what you decided back then sinks into the background of your thoughts and drives you this way or that. Then there're the disappointments and tragedies that have become unknowingly stockpiled and eventually change the direction and interrupt the flow of your self-expression too. You're just not yourself anymore. You're a version of yourself, and it's not always a version you're particularly fond of, no matter how bullish you have become about it.

You might want to pause here and give thought to what's standing in your way when it comes to love. In other words, what's your story? How do you explain the barriers between you and the other people in your life? How has your attachment to your view, your reasons and justifications that have slowly become more important, more defining than who you really are? Look, we're all human beings, we all get to experience our lives from our own little private bubble of reality, but often we'll defend that stupid little bubble all the way to divisiveness and resentment.

For what? To be right? Oh, no . . . don't tell me, to protect yourself?

I'd never diminish myself to such a degree that I'd hand all the power of who I am and what I stand for to someone else's behavior. I'm a fucking force of nature and so are you. Start acting like it.

I hate it when people set me in stone, when they basically make up their mind about me and everything I am, but it would be a bit inauthentic of me to do the same to them, wouldn't it?

You can't spend your life fighting for acceptance while never accepting others for all that they are.

That's why I make it my business to continually interrupt my stories about people and replace them with compassion and understanding. I'm in no position to judge anyone in this life, and neither the fuck are you, Pontius.

People do what they do; that's on them. I'm too busy causing my own life to find the time to step back and take the time to judge someone else's, but be left in no doubt, people become a certain way over time and it creeps up so powerfully and slowly it's hard to follow. Give understanding a try. You might surprise yourself.

Let me give you two examples at opposite extremes. There are people who can be too cold, too detached, who often hurt others with their apparent lack of affection. They'll fight for that disconnected state too. "I'm happy this way" could alternatively be heard as "I'm safer this way." The safety of isolation or ignorance hiding behind indifference. They weren't born that "way." Quite the opposite, in fact.

And on the other hand, there are those who are too affectionate, too "clingy," who smother the other party with their constant craving for attention. "I'm good, you good? We good? You're not good? I'm not good!" The anxiety of desperation. The problem is, when love is presented here, it never quite lands for that desperate soul. I mean, how could it when they've unknowingly devoted their life to coming from "no love"?

Here's a little mind bomb for you to mull over. People themselves are NEVER stuck. The only thing that's ever stuck about a person is what they talk about. We get trapped in our stories, our descriptions of life, and that kind of stuckness will only allow you to see life from a distinct viewpoint with the same predictable solutions to the same old stories over and over. You're not stuck; your talk is.

So if you're suffering from what feels like a lack of love in your life, the issue isn't "finding" love. It's not something you go out and pluck from a tree or pick up three drinks in at a bar. And no, it's not "out there" on a dating site or in the person you will throw yourself at after the current one vacates the building.

You must first look at yourself instead, to deal with what's in your way, to learn to fully express your love and to expose yourself to another's attentions and all in a mature and nurturing way. A way that works.

Use the phrases in the next chapter to guide you toward creating new mental understandings about love. When we change our perspective on love, it changes how we talk about love, it changes the stories we tell. And those change the actions we take. Watch your relationships grow and flourish in this newfound relationship to love and all that it offers.

BE LOVE

Obviously, we're not going to cover everything about love here and then suddenly you're a freaking love machine or dripping with Zen. You might already be defending your existing notion of what love is and isn't or what it should or shouldn't be. You might even be struggling to fit what I've been saying here into your current life. That's kind of the idea! If you are already becoming defensive, whatever you are defending is a big part of what has your life be the way it is. This is a place for you to start reinventing your ideas and beliefs about love. To begin forming an environment in your own head and in your life where your relationship to love is both healthy and enlivening.

Will you get disappointed with others when you choose love? Probably, yes. Will people always respond to you in the ways that you want them to? Nope. Should you use love to change them? No, but that's not love, that's using the pretense of love to produce an outcome that, in turn, makes your love inauthentic anyway. **Never** "use" love as a strategy or a weapon. Don't play those games. That's for chumps and charlatans.

Real love seeks nothing in return. It's not a burden or tainted by wants or needs. It's a magical, singular way of being that only requires an outlet, a place to be expressed, and it's on you to express that thing.

To have it burn brightly and boldly in the face of everything that life has to throw in your direction.

You don't seek love in another, you choose to *be* love with another, and it's critical that you understand and accept who you are choosing to love. It's your fucking choice. It takes real courage to love someone, to be exposed to that kind of vulnerability for the guarantee of absolutely nothing in return. But it also takes the same kind of bravery to admit that you are no longer willing to love a person, particularly without the sometimes overwhelming need to start gathering the evidence needed to blame them for your predicament.

Why should you love another? Because you can. Period.

Now, imagine that you had the love in your life really *handled*. Like you were free to express your love for people, that you were able to drop a resentment or let go of an anger or the need to be right, that you could

be open and understanding and able to intervene
with your most common, most egotistical survival
bullshit.

What if you could free yourself from judging how
others love or don't love you, from seeking approval
or transferring your needs to someone else?

What if you could just *be*? Love.

4

The Wisdom of Love

"**Love is the responsibility of the person who has it in mind.**"

We spend a lot of our adult lives holding people accountable for what *we* want. When they don't act how we want, give us what we want, it's a major problem. We have become hypnotized by our wants and needs. Lost in the backwoods of our deepest fears armed only with resignation and resentment and fueled by the bottomless pit of what we see as fair and "right." How dare they, the bunch of assholes?

In my career I've witnessed many relationships crumble simply because one person (although it's sometimes both) was continually looking to the other for the love that they themselves were after. It was a never-ending game of judgment and blame. The emotional roller coaster of "getting it-not getting it."

Think about that. Complaining (either vocally or in the quiet resentment of your own thoughts) that someone else won't give you what you want. You place the burden on them. It's now *their* job. They need to make you *feel* loved or wanted or important. The desperation and/or resignation creep in.

"You don't support me!"

"You don't love me!"

"You don't care about me!"

You may as well just scream "MAKE ME FEEL BETTER!!"

Unfortunately, this isn't quite how life works. At least it's not going to actually get you what you want in your life, which in this case is love. Seeking what you "need" in others will never fill that hole. It will always be a vacant space in the pit of your gut or the corner of your heart.

Let's uncover some bad wisdom here and a very common one at that. "Love is 50/50" or "Love is give and take," both of which will have you at various points sitting in judgment of how your partner is doing while innocently counting the number of times you are ahead. It's bad wisdom that actually divides rather than connects.

I know, I know, it all seems like a good idea. Right?

The truth is, if you don't have enough love in your life, the issue is with *you*. Always. Love is an expression, not a destination to arrive at or a trinket to somehow find and collect. You create more love in your life by *being* loving, not by seeking it in others, and if you're not satisfied with who you're *supposed* to be loving well, that's on you too. You are a self-generative phenomenon, a fucking miracle of being, remember? When you share love, that's what it is, an opportunity for you to express your love; you share it, and your ability to do so is limitless.

And you never share your love as some sort of manipulation or strategy to have others be different or play the game you want to play. You love because you can. That's it.

Now, you and I both know that a relationship becomes a whole lot easier if the person you're with understands all of this too, if they're out to express *their* love with *you*. We also know, that's simply not always the case. So what does one do if this happens? What if it becomes a one-way street?

One loves.

One loves until one is no longer willing to love, and in that single moment of time, one is courageous enough to admit it to themselves and others and to deal powerfully with the consequences of that unwillingness.

I'd like you to stew in this next part for a while. Whenever you "feel" love from another, try on the idea that it's actually you who is expressing love rather than the widely accepted notion that you are being given or are receiving it. That it's in fact you who is bringing love forth in those moments and in every moment of life when it arises until you die.

Dive in a bit here. What are the implications of this? What does this mean for you when you compare it to your real life? Where is this love coming from?

"You cannot 'have' love."

Well, there goes every rom-com ever made. Sorry, fellas.

Controversial, huh? Not really, at least not when you give yourself time to think about it.

We're each born into a life where love has been romanticized, chased, and fought over, so it's little wonder that we so readily buy into some of the more widely accepted "superstitions" about love.

That's right, superstitions.

Most of how you relate to love is about as real as the Sun rising (it doesn't do that; the Earth is moving around the Sun, remember?) or all that stuff about black cats, cracks in the sidewalk (mothers around the world just heaved a huge sigh of relief), or spilling salt and the critical need to throw a handful over your shoulder to ward off the eagerly approaching satanic beast wearing an NSYNC T-shirt. Hey, it's my devil, I get to say how they're dressed.

There are lots of things in this life that you might pursue. Money. Yes, you can kinda "have" that. A job, yes, you can technically have that too. Degrees, cars, new shoes, the body you want, the promotion you're after, etc., etc., etc.

But not love.

You cannot "have" love.

I mean come on! At the very least, where in the hell would you keep it? (Don't say in your fucking heart; I like a bit of romantic imagery as much as the next person, but the reality is your heart is just a giant organ that pulses blood.)

Love is not a target either. Why? If love is something to aim for, what does that give you in the here and now? Despair. Then you're caught in the despair/relief-from-despair trap for the next few decades of your life. Some of you have already been in that shitshow and you easily testify to its relentless drain on your aliveness.

Looking for love? FFS, STOP, DUDE!!! Haven't you been paying attention?

Use your imagination here; let yourself stew in the idea of "having" love. It's not hard to identify the presence of love, just like it's not difficult to identify the presence of anger or indifference or resentment with yourself either. What do all these things have in common? They are each experiences of your own humanity. You'll also notice that they come and go; they rise and fall, some more regularly than you'd like, others less so.

The more you release yourself from the pressure of having love, the more room you'll have to express it, and expressing love is the only kind of love you have any say in anyway. If the love in your life is a product of self-expression . . . what are the limits?

This is probably a good spot for you to do some thinking, yes?

Start with something like, "Given what I am seeing, how does this change the way I look at my past relationships and how I could approach the ones to come?"

Allow yourself the time and space to explore this notion of love on your own terms, to find a place where you can settle into it and start to live life from its promise.

"The ultimate expression of love is loving another in the way they want to be loved."

We usually love people in the way we think we're supposed to.

There's a sort of standard or model we have in mind about what love is and how it's supposed to look, and that's the model we follow in our relationships. We mostly fight about that model too. Most people don't even know they are measuring their love life against their subconscious model of how it "should be."

It's a patchwork of your own views and opinions that you've cobbled together throughout life, by watching how love played out in your family, among your friends, and in your previous relationships. There's even a big cultural influence here, with the social mores from where you grew up and even the couples from classic literature or the scripts from romance movies making their way into our ideas about how to love.

Unfortunately, the other person—you know, the one you're *supposed* to be loving—often doesn't have the exact same ideas about how this love thing is supposed to look.

Maybe you think holding hands is cheesy or sentimental, but it sets their heart aflutter. Perhaps you feel every conversation should be peppered with "I love yous" and pet names, while they think the deepest love is working sixty hours a week in their job or perhaps something unspoken or an action that doesn't, on the surface, scream "I LOVE YOU!"

Fortunately for us, there's usually plenty of overlap. In the West, for instance, almost all of us view a kiss on the lips as a romantic gesture. But there's also lots of divergence.

That's why we've all had experiences when we tried to show our love in a certain way, when we tried to do something we thought was loving but it didn't land. In the worst cases, it may have totally backfired. Because your way of loving didn't match what the other person was looking for.

Two people, two different ideas, not only of how to love, but also of how they want to actually *be* loved.

Have you ever considered that? How do you want to be loved? No really, in your closest relationship, how?

The only way to connect, to truly bond with that other person, is to express love in a way that works for them. And finding that out is as simple as asking them. It can be directly, or you can feel them out in more indirect ways to get an idea.

From there, the real challenge becomes the process of turning yourself inside out to love in the way they want. But it's a worthy challenge, because it's the only path to a strong, real relationship.

"When someone says they don't love you, it doesn't have anything to do with you."

No, really. That's all.

This is about as close to a "truth" as I could ever give you. Take this to the fucking bank. It also doesn't mean you take pity on the other person or identify with their struggle or lament your "lost opportunity."

Move on. Get back in the game. Even if they're blaming you, and they most likely will, although if it's not you, they'll point to some circumstance or mystery of the universe to explain where they are at. As always, take responsibility for your own actions;

learn from the experience; and, where appropriate, clean up your mess.

When love just isn't "there" for them, you must give up the idea that it's your job to have them see the light no matter what you've seen on TV or read in magazines. Stop looking for "clues" in their behaviors or comments too, no matter how tempting. You're putting your life on hold, delaying the magic of the future you're yet to have. Get healing and get over yourself as quickly as possible. For every person who hung in there and miraculously managed to turn a relationship around, thirty squillion others watched their lives go to hell in a handbasket under a flurry of painfully embarrassing moments; weepy nights with friends; and the occasional restraining order thrown into the mix.

Two of the reasons why people try to hang in there are because they relate to love as if it's something that is not only rare but also that it's given to them by another. Neither of these is true. There is an abundance of amazing people in this world, and you have an opportunity to express your love with all of them in a unique and satisfying way. It's rarely, if ever, the same kind of love, but that doesn't limit its potency or magic. They're all fucking great.

Love only starts to get limited when you compare one love to another. You'll never enjoy a strawberry if you keep expecting it to taste like the cheese you had before. All the loves of your life are still love.

Give them your all, and if they no longer want to share in that, shift your attention to those who do.

"The secret to love, is to love who they are."

I was almost finished writing this book—in fact, deep into the editing stage—when my mum suddenly passed away.

The urge to share something about her and her impact on me was overwhelming, and my first thought was to include these words in the "Loss" section.

That would have been a travesty and a missed opportunity for you.

You see, I was lucky. About a dozen years or so before her passing I awoke from my thirty-year pity party and took ownership of how my relationship with her was going. That new stance completely changed everything. She didn't change a thing. I did.

The problem is, most people believe they already do take ownership for their role in the relationship, although they include a steady stream of explanations as to why some of the most important relationships in their life don't work.

Start with the idea that they don't work. That you're a smaller person for this approach, that you've boxed in certain aspects of yourself you've become so accustomed to, that you're pretty convinced this isn't even a problem. It's hard to see how trapped you are until you're finally free.

Free of what? Your most precious commodity. Your point of view. The one thing in your life that you'll trash everything and anything for.

When you've finally isolated and destroyed your story, that all-too-powerful narrative of how things are/were and should be/should've been, when you confront and take responsibility for the real, in-your-face, self-inflicted damage that, uninterrupted, will live with you until the end, you are putting yourself in a very powerful place. A place of creation. Of having a real say in how all your relationships go.

And that is exactly what I did.

I chose to love my mum. All of her. Forget that bullshit about "finding positives" or "healthy boundaries," I fell head over heels in love with the idea of love and I went all in.

I chose to admire instead of resenting, I resorted to understanding over reaction, to love over all else.

And in all of it, she remained the same. Herself. No change. Her temper, her moods, her logic, and her actions. I fell in love with who she was rather than to waste my life in the complete lunacy of regret and the energy-sapping drain of who I wanted her to be. She suddenly arose right in front of my eyes. Her relentlessness, her defiance and vigor, her power and her drive.

I fell in love with the mum I had. Boom.

And that's the "secret" to love. To *fully* love who someone is, their humanity, their foibles, their past, their incompletions, and their views. You don't need to adopt any of their stuff as your stuff, you don't need to be a doormat or a victim to anything. This is all about the freedom to be you, and how you do that is by granting others the freedom to be *themselves*.

Try it out. Love who they are, all of it, and watch the drama in your life disappear into the wind.

Give yourself time to reflect on and go deeper with what we are talking about here. As a suggestion you might want to scroll back some pages to any parts that jumped out at you, do some thinking, get the notes rolling, soak this up. Remember that the words populating these pages could revolutionize not only the present but also the future. This stuff will only matter to the degree that you make it matter.

This is your opening. Make it count.

5

Loss

*You can always choose
to engage with loss
in such a way that it
empowers you rather
than smothers you.*

Just about everything you ever learned about loss is a fucking lie.

The subject has been wrapped up in a never-to-be-questioned cultural cocoon of superstition, fear, and sympathy card clichés.

Loss is most often linked to the passing of someone important in our life, whether it's a spouse, family member, friend, or even a pet. We even commonly refer to this as "losing someone," and we grieve that loss. Makes sense, right?

But there is another kind of loss that can kill off your future just as readily, although its impact is so nuanced, so creeping and invading, that you barely notice it until you're being suffocated by it. And getting over it can seem just as impossible.

The loss of a dream or situation, the death of an answer to your current predicament or situation— we actually grieve about things that were supposed to happen but didn't, for whatever reason. While it doesn't always *feel* like the darkness of "grieving," be left in no doubt that those kinds of losses have a very real and damaging impact too unless acknowledged and handled in a healthy way. Most people feel as if they can get over that stuff fairly quickly, but here's the deal: you don't. When you say "get over" what you are really saying is "I'm stuffing this down and moving onto something else," so it gets to live in the background of your thinking, shunting you this way and that, playing out in your life in ways you can't even begin to imagine. We can dwell in that shit for years too, and the impact can be catastrophic. A life put on hold or taking a wild turn or waiting for a change that ultimately never comes. Regret. Disappointment. Sometimes resentment too.

When things we wanted to have don't materialize or events we needed to occur don't come to pass, there may not be a material loss there that we can point to, but we feel that *sense* of loss nonetheless. You can eventually nest yourself there in ways that you become so accustomed to, you barely even notice how much you're still "in it." Suffering is optional, believe it or not.

Maybe your marriage or relationship hasn't gone the way you expected, perhaps it's that job or house or plan that would have solved all your shit. Maybe the dream of your best-selling book you had been longing for and fantasizing over hasn't quite manifested in the cold reality of your life, all the way down to the depths of the childhood you thought you deserved never quite matching up to the one you got.

You see there is the real, physical "loss" when someone dies, which can be painfully disempowering and all-consuming, but there is also the kind of loss where nothing tangible is gone at all. In fact, the only thing "lost" is an idea or a potential or a feeling, but nothing in real terms. People often talk about the loss of hope, for instance, when really "hope" is nothing more than a positive feeling one conjures up to help handle some current shitstorm of life. If you're someone who relies on hope to make it through your life, ditch the hope and start taking some new actions. It might be scary and hell, even painful, but it's far more likely to get the job done than the Novocain of hope you're currently applying to the most challenging parts of your life.

You might still occasionally long for a lost love, years old, like a firmly wedged blockade right in the middle of the relationship you currently have (or don't have). You spend swathes of time looking back, wondering, dreaming, comparing, and building a story, becoming more and more resigned about the life you're in and still tingling for the one you had expected or hoped for.

You, my friend, are living in a fucking fantasy. It's time to wake up.

> *The most painful state of being is remembering the future, particularly the one you'll never have.*
> —Søren Kierkegaard

GRIEVING AND GROWING

Now, to grieve is a perfectly natural part of human existence. You cannot get through this life without some sort of loss being a part of it. No chance. It's completely appropriate to grieve loss when someone dies or the end of some great hope or dream. The same with your own diminishing health or someone you love leaving. This isn't something that we need to resist. It deserves space. These emotions are all about flow. Let them through; they'll work their way out. They rise, they fall, and in between . . . life happens.

Of course, this is providing you don't try to clumsily intervene with them by adding the temporary crutch of determination or anger or resentment. Those "support emotions" will linger far longer than your real-life loss.

That being said, you do have to be responsible (aware) about how this experience plays out in your life in the longer term. Most people have zero awareness of the lingering clouds of loss in their life and how they have changed themselves in its aftermath. The changes, sometimes subtle; the results, completely life-altering.

When someone dies, for example, it's like receiving a wound. But not just any wound. This isn't as simple or surface-level as a poke, a scrape, or a cut. It's more like a mortal wound. Like it's killing you.

It's a primal gouge, a catastrophic breach of a life, a feeling that goes deep into the pit of your stomach. It's not an "ouch"; it's a subterranean moan, an existential ache that penetrates to the very root of your being. And it fucking hurts. Your emotions will plummet like a stone, you'll wonder at the point of it all. You'll hurt and struggle and, at times, feel like you're drowning in it.

How in the hell are you supposed to deal with that? What's your plan as you're tumbling through the hallways of your darkest fears and pitifully trying to stabilize yourself?

Alcohol? Work? Drugs? Staying positive? Waiting it out?

Many people adopt the positive philosophical approach of "time is a great healer" for some kind of instant relief, which inevitably results in a lifetime of checking in with yourself only to realize you're "not over it yet" and, in reality, never quite will be. For those who have ever heard that phrase in your hour of need, those paltry words made no real difference to those dense, dull moments of your greatest pain, did they?

There is, however, at least *some* kind of truth in those words. Time presents you with an opportunity. The opportunity to work out and eventually settle on where this "loss" will be located for you. Will it nurture you? Perhaps it will cripple you. The good news is you have a say in that.

For a great many people, it ends up somewhere detrimental, somewhere in their subconscious that causes them to occasionally but regularly focus on it, to get stuck in the constant cycle of lamenting a loss. When you grieve like this, when you have let loss settle into you in a negative way, it ties you permanently to your past. You'll never be free this way. Never. Time can't help you there either.

"I'll never get over this." That's right.

But there's another option. You see, the reason why grief is such a natural part of our lives is that it serves a purpose. Grieving loss authentically doesn't hold you back. And it doesn't matter whether it's the heavy weight of someone dying or the panic of losing a job or the despair of missing an opportunity. While it may feel painful at first, in the end it could actually empower and sometimes even enliven you.

When I think back on loved ones who have passed (I don't say "lost" when talking about people who have died, as the constant use of that language will leave you with only loss), when something I see or hear reminds me of them and I find their willowy memory in my mind's eye, I allow myself the temporary experience of grief. It rises and I allow its presence to be with me. I don't resist, I don't try to change or be more philosophical or, God forbid, turn that fucking frown upside down. No. I allow it. It's okay. I don't wallow in it, either, I let it pass through unhindered, and then I return to life.

I also don't focus at all on what "could/should have been," as that's all just fantasy now and, to be quite honest, a safe little spot where I can deny responsibility for how my life is going. I'm just not interested in anything that takes my hands off the wheel of where my life is headed, even for a moment or ten. I let go of the urge to begin longing for their presence or cursing fate or disease or age. I certainly don't dwell on how much I loved them in the past tense or indulge "missing" them either. None of that serves who they still are for me OR for the life I have right now.

Instead, it's an experience of warmth, of being nurtured by them in this very moment. I think of how much I love them right now. It's a love I'm currently experiencing, that I continue to feel, rather than something that suddenly ceased or changed with their passing. Who they are lives on and on with every memory. To me, their life lives on in me and that will only end when I do.

There's no loss in the sense of the word I had so long accepted as true but rather a transformation of the relationship I had into the one I now have.

Because of this, they are always alive for me; their memory doesn't make me feel as if there's something missing, as if there's a part of me that's gone and can't be replaced. Rather, my love for them gives me a sense of fullness, of wholeness, that adds to my life rather than subtracts.

CHOOSE TO BE EMPOWERED

Put yourself in this location right now. For loss of any kind to serve you, it has to be something you can look back on and find a way to use it to empower yourself. It's not about overcoming loss, it's about repositioning it, of allowing it to settle into the background of your life and occasionally surface to remind you of who you are and who you've been.

When I think back on the death of my father, I don't feel any despair now. But, of course, it wasn't always like this. There was a period when I was choked by the thick black smoke of shock and grief, when I felt as if

I could no longer breathe with the wave of emotion after emotion, when I first began to face a life with someone so close to me no longer being physically there. There was a hole where he used to be, and I experienced the deep hopelessness of the need to fill that hole with something. Anything. After a single, stiff whiskey (I don't even like whiskey, I know, sacrilege, right?), I did the kind of thinking you're reading here.

I read, I talked to whoever would listen, I worked, I meditated until . . . click. I eventually owned my experience. It was mine and I'm responsible for it. I healed.

Most people have no idea of the work that needs to be done, so they have no choice but to leave that hole open, gaping to the universe and ultimately distressing. Some become fatally tainted by that experience, hardened or emotionally burdened by it, both of which are options, not fate.

All of what I'm saying here isn't just something I already knew or some genetic trait I have. I had to learn this through the chaos of the situation and my willingness to read, hear, think, and apply new knowledge. I literally caused my own breakthroughs, just as you can.

Let me be clear about one thing, however. Whether it's for six months, a year, or two years, you must always allow yourself the space to grieve fully, but there is a "sell by" date. *No one* gets to tell you when that date is. It's something only you can decide on, and it'll depend on your own temperament, your relationship to the person/situation, your philosophy on life, and other factors that are unique to you. But there will be a point where that grief is going beyond its usefulness, when it's no longer serving a real purpose. Where it's taking you and your life down or being used as a weapon to justify your current existence.

You must guard against the sneaky bastard of self-indulgence.

Often you can identify the expiration date of your loss by the number of times you're now using to explain or excuse yourself. When it's now become your go-to with friends or the press of your job or family or life itself. And well you know: they'll never mess with that card whenever you choose to play it. Don't think for a moment that people won't play that game, because they do. Your job is to make sure you're not that person.

But when that time of "enough" comes, you have to be ready to do the work to center yourself, to relocate that grief to a place where it strengthens rather than weakens you.

It won't be easy. Loss can be a tough thing to deal with. There are some people whose life is never quite the same after going through it, who are changed forever. A life of disappointment and what could have been.

That doesn't have to be you.

You can always choose to engage with that loss in such a way that it empowers you rather than smothers you.

6

The Wisdom
of Loss

"**The only stuff you can't get over is the stuff you're holding on to.**"

Ouch, right? People could easily react to this quote with a heavy dose of outrage. And I get it.

Why is that? Well, two things. First, the very topic of loss is often a societally forbidden subject unless approached with the extreme care of a nuclear reactor core. It's "no go" zone for many people. The kind of safe place where they can retreat and where no one can follow them. People often slip into the trap of doing the same when it comes to their bodies or their health. It can all too easily become an escape from the press of life. I mean, you just don't mess with someone when they say, "I'm sick/depressed/grieving, back the hell off!," do you? No, no one does.

Second, most people have little or no idea that they are holding on to stuff from their own past. In their mind, it seems like there is something clinging to *them*.

In my life, I've experienced lots of loss. And I've coached many people who have too.

When you're writhing in the throes of loss, when you're in the grip of that intense feeling of emptiness, you feel like you don't have a say. That you're at the mercy of this thing and that you have no say in how this goes.

And so it's pretty damn annoying when people tell you to "cheer up" or to "let it go" because it just seems like you can't, right?! I mean, no one would be doing this to themselves!

Maybe.

Again, I get it. If you feel yourself starting to get angry or defensive at this time, rein it in and think with me for a moment. There's something here for you.

Of course, this also includes those who already realize that the aftermath of their loss has been going on a little (or a lot) too long now, is still too intense, or is playing a bigger role in their life than they think it should by now.

Ask yourself the following:

> *"What kind of life do I get to live with this loss continuing?"*

> *"What do I get to excuse myself from with this loss?"*

"If I could no longer talk about this loss, what would I have to face about my life?"

Among your answers to those questions is what you are hanging on to. It will also include what you are avoiding, and justifying too. Now, I appreciate that this might be an uncomfortable item for you to face. It's okay, you can do this. You can turn the tables on yourself so you come roaring out the other side and are ready to take your life on again.

Many of us attach loss to the things in life that we're not doing. We fall into this rut of, "I'm not going to do X, Y, or Z because I'm dealing with A." We make these subconscious connections as an outlet so we don't have to be with what we think life will be after the loss. We say, "I'm drinking a lot . . . but I can't get over ___." Or "I'm putting on weight . . . but it's because of the divorce." Or "There's a problem in my relationship . . . but it's because my mom died."

But these things aren't connected. You connected them.

Yes, intense loss might expose someone to the *idea* that drinking is a solution. Or eating. Or distancing themselves from people in their lives and shutting it down. But one is not "caused" by the other. When you start insisting on the idea that these are caused phenomena you completely take yourself out of being the solution. It's like you can throw your helpless hands in the air and check out and there's not a soul in your life who can touch you because it's not your fault. The problem is, this isn't about fault or who's to blame. No one cares about that. It's irrelevant now.

This is all about what's next. About life after loss, and it's never as bleak as the picture in your mind. No matter how painful, no matter how debilitating it seems.

You can still live your life while grieving. You can still go to work, go to the gym, spend time with your family. The loss doesn't have to consume you. It doesn't have to drag you down or hold you back or send your life off in a direction from which you'll never recover. Sure, you need space; sure, you need compassion and understanding, but you also need a future, a life where you have learned to be with that loss so that you can explore life at new levels.

"Today is also one of those days you'll never get back."

We often watch people or situations as they slip from our lives, and the dark sense of regret, coulda, shoulda, woulda, becomes heavy and constraining over time.

We experience the loss, feel the absence, and yet continue living in the same way we were before. Nothing really changes. We're just sadder or more deflated or lost. Sometimes anger or resentment moves in.

Of course, this isn't the case for everyone. For some, the experience of loss is like an epiphany. They realize "What the fuck am I doing?" and turn their whole life around. They change careers, take control of their health, or simply choose to become a new person almost entirely.

But there are ways in which any of us can refocus grief so it works for us like that. Where it moves beyond a few tears or regrets and manifests itself in real, positive thoughts and actions.

And there's no better way, in my opinion, than confronting your own death. Use the actuality of your death to help you come to grips with your own mortality.

Believe it or not, you're going to die one day. Maybe it's tomorrow. Maybe it's fifty years from now. If you can really take ahold of that, there's no bigger fire you could light under your ass. And we're rarely as close to our own death as when someone close to us passes.

There's a magic and a power when you're able to take that situation, the death of a loved one or even an acquaintance, and reconfigure it so it inspires you. And the above is just one example.

After my father died, my go-to was to think, *How would **he** feel about how I'm living my life?*

That one was a real slap in the face, a real wake-up call, my "What the fuck am I doing?" moment. It changed the trajectory of where my life was going.

And change begins in a single moment. You can start today. You can begin that moment *now*.

We often think of change as something that happens over time. And there is an element of truth to that. But what we're really seeing in those situations is a series of changes. They're lots of little alterations that started with one pivotal moment.

This could be that moment. This could be your day. And the death that you experienced, the grief that you're feeling, could be the spark that starts the fire that propels you forward. It's just a matter of changing the way you look at it.

What would that change look like?

❝It's okay you're overwhelmed. It's appropriate, not permanent.❞

When confronted by loss, many of us have that experience of complete and utter overwhelming.

Life's too much, too heavy, too complicated. You can't face your problems; hell, you can hardly even face getting out of bed! No amount of motivation or stimulation can seem to pierce through the lethargy, the noise, or the helplessness.

Now, there are certain times when overwhelming can be a sign that you're taking on a bigger life and you're at the point of being unable to handle that expansion. In that case, you cannot keep doing things the way you are used to. You might need to outsource some of your commitments or take another look at how you approach your life. One thing's for sure: you cannot expect to be you AND expand.

However, when it comes to loss, being overwhelmed can just take the legs out from you. It seems like a completely different kind of overwhelming, and therefore a distinct and unique strategy is required, no?

No. Not quite.

The biggest reason why people struggle with being overwhelmed is that at some level they feel as if they're not supposed to be this way. That we're supposed to be somehow different. I mean, come on, this is a horrible feeling and needs to go away! Maybe some meditation or rest or getting our house in order will do the trick, right? Maybe.

Ultimately, people struggle with the feeling of being overwhelmed more than they do with the things that had them feel that way in the first place. Read that part again.

Kinda like being depressed about being depressed.

Of course, most people don't do the same with the feeling of happiness. They don't lift their voice to the sky and yell, "Why me? Why am I so happy?" when everything's going great in their life. But the moment their plate starts to fill, they start to agitate, to complain, to take up their unspoken resistance against what is, even though it makes absolutely no difference to what is going on.

In some cases it only worsens an already crappy experience.

You see, in certain times in your life, especially times when you are experiencing the loss of a person or a dream, it's not only expected that you might get overwhelmed, it's also completely appropriate. You're supposed to feel this way whenever you're at your limits. Of course, there'll be pushback and you'll get that heavy feeling of being incapable or lost or whatever your thing is. It's okay.

With that in mind, the answer to those feelings of being overwhelmed is not to fight or wrestle with them. Let go of your automatic need to struggle or, at the other end of the spectrum, hide. The key here is to accept where you are. The answer is to realize it's okay to be overwhelmed. Those feelings will come and go, and sure, you'll get stressed, a little flustered, maybe even a bit fucked up, but you'll survive. Take care of your well-being, do whatever you need to nurture and nourish yourself, but it's also okay to push on a bit too.

And it's not going to last forever. There's a time limit. Eventually you'll either overcome the shit you're dealing with, or you'll get so used to dealing with it that you don't even break a sweat doing it.

This chapter might have been a hard one for you. Remember, as I said earlier, take a breath, go for a walk, do something to connect to the present and remind yourself what you're here for. What you're doing this for. Becoming aware of what is really true about how we navigate these difficult situations of loss can empower us, remember? That's no small thing. In fact, it's huge.

7

Fear

To fear is to be alive. It's your job to understand that and to push past it.

Boo! Scared yet?

If you ask anyone why they feel as if they're stuck or trapped, why they don't reach for greatness or break out of a crumbling life and you question a little, they all initially cough up the same boring answer to that existence of predictability and beigeness.

Fear.

They'll say it's a fear of failure or judgment or rejection or whatever. But is that really it? Is that all? You're just shit scared? At some level all people, you included, have built a life around your fears rather than your potential. What's recognized as safe over the magic of what's possible.

You don't ask for that raise because you fear you might not get it. You don't ask that person out because you're afraid they'll say no. You don't start a business or write that book or apply to that college or even go to the gym because . . . what's the fucking point, right? I mean, you'll only fail again, won't you?

And when you do . . . what will they all think?

And that dead and flattened valley where you find yourself after you fail is so bad, so depressing, so painfully exposed, so devoid of the safe cover under which you usually operate, it's small wonder you're more than a little hesitant about baring your most sensitive self to that shit again. When you do fail, it's always a familiar, sometimes crippling button that gets pushed. One that confirms something you'd always known but would rather not deal with.

And when that gets revisited . . . the illusion is that the whole world will see your charade. The game you've been playing to hide some dark, deep truth about not being good enough or not lovable or not smart or . . . you get the picture. Your life is always a manifestation, in real time, of what you're painfully trying to hide behind the mask.

So we stop at fear. We give in to the paltry explanation, which is why fear is the most commonly used word to explain or excuse a life. Even in the workshops I've facilitated, the group agreement for fear is tangible and often argued for. People will back each other's fears up and demand their right to live a life of fear without ever really examining the cost of such a thing.

But in reality, it's a misplaced fear. Truthfully, there's nothing to be afraid of. Well, not a lot, let's put it that way.

Sure, there are some things to be legitimately scared of. If you're swimming in the ocean, basking in the quiet satisfaction and bliss of nature and then start to hear the dull, growing tones of the *Jaws* theme music accompanied by a soft swish of the water behind you, okay, I think most people would say it's appropriate to be afraid. However, be sure to check before you start screaming for your life, as it's most likely a random cello player on vacation splashing next to you.

Sharks can't play stringed instruments.

In short, if your existence is genuinely at risk, sure, it's natural to feel fear. Appropriate, even. In those cases, all the time, every time, honor your safety.

But that's not what we're dealing with here, is it?

In this case, we don't fear because something is life-threatening. We're simply using "fear" as a Band-Aid to cover everything we don't want to face. It's an explanation that allows us to put that task off indefinitely.

But I want you to rip that Band-Aid off. Dig down a little into this fear to find out what's really down there.

"Ah, Gary, I know what it is. It's a fear of failure!"

That's the popular social media answer these days, isn't it? There have got to be a billion Instagram posts equating our fear of action with a fear of failure, complete with an overplayed quote from a success story that tells us why they've never been afraid of failure.

And hey, I'm not saying there's anything particularly wrong with that. But I will say that it's not going deep enough.

Look, your problem is not a fear of failure itself, but a fear of being *seen* to fail. In other words, if no one ever knew you had failed, if no one saw or heard or witnessed your plunge from grace, you wouldn't care as much, if at all. Keep in mind that this equation also includes you. Even if you're alone, your aversion to failure is because "you" will still know that you failed.

That's why kids can get into all kinds of weird stuff without a care in the world. Those of you who have witnessed your child's first steps into the world of "dressing" themselves will testify to their blatant don't-give-a-fuck-ness about how they appear to others. Because not only do they not care what people think, they are only ever trying to impress themselves.

What do you think of them? Ha! Who cares?

So it's not a fear of failure that's stopping you but rather a desire to avoid being judged, both by yourself and others, that's holding you back. That's what has you rolling out those ready-made excuses and explanations that seemingly are impeding your pathway. But it's not the explanation that stops you. It's what's behind that little story of yours—and what's behind that is your ever-present concern for how you are seen, or rather who you are seen to *be*.

That's why you make the story so compelling. It must be so absolute, so impossible, so real and heavy that others will readily believe it. And that's the unspoken trade we have with each other. Agree with my shit and I'll agree with yours. Then we can become great friends and cop out of life together.

Then your story becomes the truth. Then you start to be burdened by your cop-out life while reading books and taking advice and getting depressed and attempting to change so that you might eventually stumble upon the luck or mystery of the universe or whatever, that will make it all better. That's right, you start trying to make your cop-out life better. That's the limit of it all. To make the suffering sufferable.

How do you end this sufferable cycle? You start by paying attention to your internal experience of fear, not what you're doing. What does it feel like when you're afraid? Think about the specific and familiar thoughts, feelings, and emotions that accompany your fear. Do you start to sweat? Does your heart race?

Once you recognize what it looks like, then you can start putting things into perspective. You can learn to live *with* fear without using it as an excuse. It's not about being fearless but rather realizing that you're okay with it. You've accepted it. It's not about avoiding being judged but instead realizing that all people will judge, and it is far better to be judged for who you are rather than something you're pretending to be, designed to keep you in a predictable, safe little box.

Yeah, you're being judged. So fucking what? You've been judging me (or what I've written) since you started reading this book! Get over yourself. You're doing fine. Step the hell up.

As Kierkegaard said, "To venture causes anxiety, but not to venture is to lose one's self . . . And to venture in the highest is precisely to be conscious of one's self."

In other words, to venture, to take action, is going to cause some level of fear, possibly even anxiety, and the farther you take it, the more self-conscious you'll be, and the more fear you'll experience. But it's not life-threatening. And that fear is supposed to be there. To fear is to be alive.

It's your job to understand that and to push past it.

Let's be honest. Most people today live pretty safely. They work in an air-conditioned building, drive a car with all the safety checks and features, and acquire sanitized food with a shopping cart and a credit card, not charging through the woods with a bloodied spear or against the harshness of the elements with a plow. In short, most of this fear stuff is bullshit. It's not stopping you from doing anything. It's more like anxiety over your self-consciousness, not a legitimate fear over something life-threatening.

We all feel fear. But it's not an excuse not to take action.

8

The Wisdom of Fear

FUNDAMENTAL #1

"Your fear is meaningless."

There is no fear in the universe. It doesn't exist.

It's as real as boredom or willpower, and no, just because something feels real to you doesn't make it real outside of the confines of your own little world.

You might be one of those people who has been stuck for months or even years by the presence of fear. You've cashed in your aliveness and potential for relief from those sweaty palms, racing thoughts, elevated heartbeat, and plunging loss of personal power. But your fear is meaningless too.

Fear is nothing more than a temporal experience for a human being when faced with the random, chaotic shit thrown in the way of a life and blown dramatically out of proportion until it becomes far more significant than it is in reality.

Your fear is meaningless: it has no preloaded significance or importance. It's an empty cup that you fill with whatever explosive, unstable load that eventually derails you.

Fear is now a giant cosmic joke, one that, once upon a time in our evolutionary history, was deadly serious and designed to help you survive a wild and dangerous planet, except you're now trying to survive a meeting or an interview or a date or a career change or saying something you've been meaning to say but somehow can't bring yourself to.

And it can become so woefully misplaced that you are quite literally bringing your entire life to a standstill.

That stomach-churning, knee-trembling, thought-charging, palm-softening, life-threatening grip that catches us all unprepared. And for many of us, it happens way more often than we'd like. But just because the experience is real doesn't mean what you think it does.

Think about this. Is asking someone out on a date the exact same kind of scary to everyone? How about requesting a raise or going to the gym or telling someone how you feel? Public speaking, anyone?

There's nothing about those things that will actually hurt us. That's why there are so many people who can do them with little more than a deep breath and a "here we go." But why, then, are others completely frozen to the spot?

Because you are not driven by your fear of something but rather you get twisted out of shape by your hidden *relationship* to that thing. You're not afraid of public speaking, for instance (and you can insert the things in your life you're afraid of here), you're afraid of what you have made public speaking mean; and what you have made it mean is hidden from your view.

You are the architect of fear. It's coming from you, and your blind insistence that you should somehow *not* be fearful only reinforces that fear.

Somewhere in your mind, at some point in your life, in the momentary background of your thoughts, the question was asked, "What does this mean to me?" And you came up with an answer that fit your circumstances, who you were being at the time. In those moments, you came up with some story about yourself that, if you were to speak to a group, would be painfully exposed for all to see. Is it any wonder you are rooted to the spot, mumbling and shuffling your little reminder cards, trying to hide your internal drama from the onlookers? That's the problem with these kind of stories; they're not stories to you. In your mind, your story is as real as it gets.

But fear grips us in all kinds of different ways.

Some people love dogs. They're "man's best friend," after all, right? Yet others recoil at the sight of even the friendliest of golden retrievers, all because they were bit or surprised or intimidated by some neighborhood dog when they were a kid and now . . . the story is a fully fledged three-part drama that has taken over the prime-time slot of their life.

In short, fear isn't about you. It's about that weight or significance you've come up with about that thing and added to the mix. In fact, fear doesn't even really exist in the world. It's not tangible. You can't reach out and touch it. You can't pick it up or hold it.

But we feel it. We feel it deeply, we experience it viscerally. It grips us.

Yet all of the fear in your life is entirely of your making. As such, it's not something to be fought against. It's something to coexist with, to live your life alongside of, without trying to resist it at every step of the way.

It's a human experience.

If fear was a set thing, if it was immutable or immovable, then everybody on a roller coaster would experience the exact same thing. But they don't. One person is thinking what a mistake it was to let their friends talk them onto the ride, as they grip the bars holding them in like their life depends on it. Another is having the time of their life, with a massive grin plastered on their face.

This is the case for all fear. It's subjective. Different people experience it in different ways over different things.

You might fear public speaking, while your colleague revels in it. You might live for the gym or for competitive sports, while your best friend withers away at the mere thought of it.

Why? Because it's not what you're actually doing that you fear, it's something else. It's the significance, the weight, or as Sartre would say, the meaning that you've attached to that action or event.

Give that some thought. All the ways you have made certain things in your life be far bigger than they really are, particularly when driven by that overblown sense of fear that shows up from time to time. You can either be driven by that fear or declare yourself big enough to bring it along for the ride. Fear can be the companion or the driver; that choice will be yours.

"The line between compassion for yourself and self-pity can disappear without warning."

We all get caught in the grip of fear at some point or other.

And fear doesn't have to mean spine-tingling, piss-your-pants terror. For some, fear often comes in the form of anxiety or worry. We feel anxious when we're dealing with something that is too much or too unknown or too risky.

Fear mixed with the internal dialog of *I can't do it* often results in retreat and the logic of safety.

As a potential prescription for dealing with these situations, there's a lot of bad wisdom that tells us things such as "give yourself a break" or "don't be so hard on yourself." In other words, the remedy, we're told, is to back off, to pull back, to stop pushing ourselves.

And there's sometimes a lot of value in that. I can't say that strongly enough, because sometimes we really are too hard on ourselves and sometimes we really do need to give ourselves a break. However, I've found those kinds of human beings to be in the minority, with the majority *believing* they're too hard on themselves when, in fact, they're just not. The slightest twinge of pain, discomfort, or impatience and **bam** . . . they're out of the game.

At the same time, you have to be aware. You have to be responsible that you don't back off to the point that you're paralyzed, that you don't "take it easy" on yourself until you're not even moving forward at all. That you surrender to something subconscious rather than pressing into some new idea or self-expression. Most human beings, wrestling with the notion of significant life change, will have to push through something they either hadn't planned for or desired. Freedom lies on the other side.

Like most things in life, I see fear as a spectrum. And self-compassion is on a sliding scale too.

If you don't keep tabs on it, that self-compassion, when in the grips of fear, can slip right on down the line into self-pity before you even know what hit you. You go from giving yourself a break, to giving yourself an excuse. From cheering yourself up, to living in complete denial of what you're dealing with.

It's the difference between *I don't think I can do this*, referring to a particular task or situation, and *I can't do anything*, as if you're worthless or the world is out to get you.

An easy way to tell if you've started to fall into the latter category is to take stock of how frequently you're "giving yourself a break." If this is a constant thing, if you're taking a "break" day after day or week after week, you probably are—or are in danger of—getting trapped in that self-pity zone of paralysis.

People who pause in the self-pity zone don't see themselves that way. They don't see themselves as victims, but they are, regardless of how feisty or in control they might seem on the outside.

You think other people do these things, but not you.

If that's you, or you'd like to avoid it becoming you, then instead of always backing off, you might need to step in. Sometimes what we need is not to be easier on ourselves, but to push through that adversity, to hold our own feet to the fire and see what we're made of.

Otherwise you're liable to get stuck in that cycle, hosting a pity party for yourself, where you're the only one invited. And the worst kind of victim is the one who thinks they aren't one.

"To fear is to be human; to avoid fear is to avoid your own humanity."

There's kind of a two-headed nature to fear. On one hand, we try our best to avoid it. And yet we're inexplicably drawn to it at the same time.

Think of a roller coaster. Many of us will save for months, endure a road trip across the country in a crowded car full of our grumpy family members, then stand in line for half an hour, only to scare ourselves silly on the biggest and baddest roller coaster we can find. I mean, it's scary but it's safe . . . right?

At times we do everything we can to avoid fear, but then we'll go to great lengths to experience fear in the next moment, provided it's in an environment that we feel some control over. Why else would horror movies be so popular?

Of course, not everyone likes roller coasters. Or horror movies. And not everyone is drawn to fear. Some of us avoid it at all costs. We'll spend the whole day inside, in our bedroom or living room, trying to stay away from even the potential, the chance of fear.

Because at some level, we feel that fear needs to be avoided. That we shouldn't visit fear too often. That it's too uncertain and unsettling.

So we do things to deal with it, to help us overcome or ignore it. That could be popping a few pills to temporarily quiet your experience or meditating, drinking, smoking pot, whatever lessens that feeling of fear, to dampen the jitters when you feel anxious in social situations or are gripped by the worries of this month's bills. Or again, we simply avoid it. We'll shy away from anything that invades our little bubble of safety and security.

If you're anxious in social situations, for instance, maybe you avoid parties, crowds, or romantic relationships simply because of the possibility that you'll end up in an awkward or uncomfortable situation. One that you don't think you can handle.

It could be connected to academic or intellectual pursuits too. You avoid writing that essay, reading that book, taking that course, because you fear it. Or you put off starting that business, asking for that raise, pushing for that sale—again, apparently because of fear.

But here's the thing. Fear has nothing to do with you. It's not a fault, a weakness that only you have. In fact, it's as natural as your hair growing. It's an essential, unavoidable piece of your humanity.

And the things you have in mind in life, those goals you've set, dreams you've thought up, if you want to actually accomplish them, you'll have to do them alongside fear.

Pay attention to the word "alongside." You are not a fearful person. Again, it's not about you. But the fear is there, and you are operating alongside it, independent, aware, and taking full responsibility for the ways in which you will predictably check out when the fear kicks in. When you are victorious with fear, you are someone who can act in its presence and are in complete ownership of your experience. Having fear is not the problem; the problem is when the fear has *you*.

Stop trying to make it go away and instead own it as yours and step out there anyway. Your life awaits.

9

Success

*Who you **are** is successful. The thing that you're chasing, you already are that thing. Right here, right now. It's not about becoming anything but rather using this moment of time to express who you already are.*

I'm fucking sick of success. No, really.

At least the way it is portrayed in most modern societies these days. It's a complete scam that we've all unknowingly bought into in one way or another. It's not that I'm sick of *being* successful. I'm sick of people being shown a bait-and-switch pathway to happiness, only to be duped time and again.

Success and happiness are two distinct phenomena that never should be confused. Do so at your peril.

On one hand, everyone is looking for peace of mind and fulfillment and the never-ending wisp of being present to the magic of being alive while simultaneously being stuck in a mindless race to some distant day in the future when it's all supposed to miraculously turn out. So peace of mind, fulfillment, and presence are cashed in right now in exchange for worry, anxiety, being overwhelmed, and the temporary high of eventually "making it" someday. How mental is that?

Success is a tired and painfully boring topic of thousands of books, seminars, philosophies, schemes, and strategies. It seems we're all chasing stupid success in one form or another. Even those who say they aren't chasing success, that they're not in the "rat race," are pursuing their own version of success, just not in a way that is easily identifiable to themselves. It's often done as a petty rebellion against society or parents or "the man," whoever that may be.

The desire for less can be just as consuming as the desire for more.

But what is "success" really? More importantly, what is it for you? How would you know if you had even been successful? More money? Less stress? Travel?

Sure, you and I may have very different visions or definitions of success, but ultimately, success implies a certain level of consensus, of relation to the people and the world around us.

In short, we have a general agreement in this society of what success is and isn't. Even if only a hundred other people agree with your particular version of success, that's still agreement. But agreement does not equal reality. Most of your life is spent in complete servitude to whichever agreed reality you've stuck yourself with.

Everybody's trying to get "there" in complete arrogance and ignorance that there is no "there." It's an illusion. A scam. There's only ever "here." There is only one time: this time. No past, no future, only this, and if you can't wake up to this, you're forever asleep. You're a fucking robot.

Your life is a series of "nows" and then you die. That's it. Everything else is just brain patterns and old emotions and behaviors. If you can't be happy/satisfied/fulfilled now, then when? Later? OMFG are you even paying attention? Get your eyes and ears on your real-real-real reality, the one that's right in front of your face right now.

As I like to say, you're always "here," but are you ever really here for what's here?

Are you here to love, to forgive, to risk, to be, to do, to express what's possible and all in this very moment of time? I mean, for fuck's sake, what other moment do you think you have?

Think of all the "moments" you have lost with resentment, anger, procrastination, cynicism, gossip, daydreaming—you name it. If you added all those moments up, what could you have done with that time? When you are facing the end of your life, those wasted moments will be what you are left with, what you could have done, who you should have been.

I'm not even blaming you here. You got duped, suckered like the rest of us, and at some level you already knew it but went along with the charade anyway.

In the West, most of our hypnotic ideas of success, whether it's the most mainstream or the most niche, essentially boil down to some form of materialism or other, and all modeled around the notion that once you get to your goal, all your shit will turn out. Ha!!

It won't.

Because even if it does, you'll be seduced into trying to get to another "there." Just like you did before. The hamster wheel isn't what you're doing. *You're* the fucking hamster wheel.

Your goals of a high-earning career, mansion, a luscious, sexy partner, or the "freedom" to do what you want. It's all about more, higher, faster, and better. In recent years, we've seen the trend swing in the other direction, to minimalism, tiny homes, and Teslas. The kind of life that could catapult your Instagram dreams. It's the "less is more" version of success. Opposite ends of a spectrum but still, essentially, the same mode to get there. We are all driven to get to the end of the rainbow. Pick an end and off you go.

Always going somewhere but never truly here. The problem is, "here" is where "it's" at.

Think.

Both the maximalist and the minimalist camps are materialistic in that they view success as a phenomenon that exists somewhere in the universe. While that corporate CEO and/or your neatly tattooed barista may appear totally different at first glance, may seem to talk about and value totally different things, they're more than likely still alternate views coming from the same window.

Whether you buy a car based on horsepower or gas mileage, you're still buying a car. Even the folks biking or walking to work aren't excluded. It's all just your version of "better."

Not only do most of us view success as external, we also tend to project it into the future. It's often something that happens later, when we've advanced enough in our career or put enough hours in at the gym. Even if we've already achieved a lot of the things we've set out to do, there's typically still some kind of better success we're working toward that's still one, five, or ten years away.

It's losing X amount of pounds, making X amount of dollars, reading X number of books, or paying off X amount of debt.

In short, whatever your version of success, it's almost always external and later. And you've bought into it. Completely.

And even though society can impact our views of what success looks like, many people run all the way to victimhood by complaining that they've been conditioned, that they've been forced or tricked into these ideas about success, that they've been brainwashed into valuing things they don't really value.

You may as well have a giant neon sign above your head proclaiming, "It's not me, it's THEM!"

Puh-fucking-lease!!!

There's no shadowy group of people trying to condition little old you. There are simply a series of spoken and unspoken agreements in society, any society, on what's good and bad, and you have chosen to go along with them. It's the same story everywhere in the world—though someone in Japan may have a slightly different version of success in mind than someone in, say, Brazil.

This means that you can't blame anyone but yourself for how you currently view and interact with success, and your rebellion against it is actually evidence of your continued buy-in to it.

Aren't you getting this yet? You see, all of this now means you can decide to change it. You can stop buying into the external and someday-later version of success.

You can replace it with something more fulfilling. Life is not a fucking treadmill. It's a garden. One to be created and nurtured and enjoyed and, like all gardens, it's sometimes work and effort too, but if you cannot bring yourself to love the work, you'll never truly love the garden.

Now, this may sound a little cliché, but I believe that "it's not where you're going, it's where you are."

Success isn't something down the street or two months away. It's who you are. Who you *are* is successful. The thing that you're chasing, you already are that thing. Right here, right now. It's not about becoming anything but rather using this moment of time to express who you already are. Results? Oh, they'll come, my friend, they'll come because you are the real deal and your actions are always aligning with who you are but you have no anxiety or worry or pressure because you are always here for what's here, and as long as you take that approach, the future takes care of itself!

> *Man is the only creature who*
> *refuses to be what he is.*
> —*Albert Camus*

This doesn't mean that you stop reaching, that you stop trying to improve yourself. But the reach is no longer desperate. It's the kind of reach that inspires the life you have.

You can be content with who you are and still reach for great things. But it's no longer the reach of a drowning man grasping for a life preserver. It's the reach of someone planted firmly in the boat or on the shore, with a firm foundation for and a confidence in where they are.

10

The Wisdom
of Success

"When the responsibility for the quality of your life lies with anyone but you, you become the victim."

This shit will probably be on my gravestone.

This statement is such a foundational piece for everything I do. If you've read any of my books or followed me online, this will sound very familiar. And if you simply cannot or will not reconcile this for yourself, you should try another route, as I'm definitely not your guy. If you're struggling to reconcile this for yourself, that's fine; we can at least work with that. Your struggle points to at least *some* degree of willingness on your part.

If your answer to being responsible for your life starts with,

"Yeah, but you never had a mom who . . ."

Or

"Sure, but my ex . . ."

Or

"Nice concept, but what about reality, Gary?"

Your bankruptcy, abuse, loss, abandonment, being taken advantage of, being duped, being stalked, place of birth, sexuality, health, weight, age, physical appearance, struggle, character flaw—you name it—none of it will ultimately determine how your life will go as long as you start with the idea that this is now unavoidably and inextricably on YOU. All in, no kidding.

Not your part in it, no "yeah, but" or "what if" either.

We've all got our heads wired up to automatically spin things as soon as they go wrong, so this isn't personal to you. Whether you're vocal about who did it or you squirrel your opinion away for later use, it's all the same. The second when shit gets off track, we're searching for who fucked it up. The desire to blame is lightning quick and will suck the power right out of you.

A deal fell through. Whir. "It's all John's fault." Someone forgot to bring the potato salad to the barbecue. Whir. "Honey, I thought you were supposed to grab it."

Over the course of our lives, we become so good, so automatic at this that we can figure out exactly who's to blame for any and all of our problems, from the flat tire we got on the way to work, to our depleted checking account, to the crappy boss who passed you over for that promotion, and all in the blink of an eye.

Haven't you ever wondered what all this plate-spinning is doing to you?

You see, while you're actively and consistently absolving yourself of ownership, you're subtly taking away your own power to do anything significant about the mess you're in. You're taking the steering wheel of your life and placing it in something or someone else's hands, giving them control. Meanwhile, you're in the back seat sighing and rolling your eyes when your life inevitably takes shitty turn after shitty turn.

Blaming people for the things that happen or happened in your life doesn't resolve them. Finding someone to point the finger at doesn't fix anything. Good luck with waiting for that apology too; even if you eventually do get it, it most likely won't do a thing for you, no matter how much you've convinced yourself it will.

Now, this doesn't mean you never hold other people accountable when they legitimately screw up. But if you're going to be successful, you've got to find a way to place yourself at the center of your own little universe.

You have to shift your perspective, to place the responsibility fully on your own shoulders, to stop pretending you're a victim of your circumstances and surroundings.

Responsibility begins with, "This happened. Now what?" If the answer to that question leaves you hanging, keep looking until you can see yourself not only at the source of your issue but also with a pathway as to how you're going to get out of it.

If you want the praise and glory when things go right—money, respect, recognition—then you've got to learn to take the crap too and not just some of it, all of it. Why? Because when you take full responsibility for how this is going it's now upon you to find answers, to seek resolution and clarity.

Occasionally it's going to take some mental acrobatics for you to get there too. Again, most of us have been playing this spin game our whole lives, so you'll need to do some rewiring to overcome that instinct. You might even begin to realize how much of a victim you have become during this process, how quickly you turn to helplessness or resignation as a pathway to giving up.

Here's what I need you to know. You can do this. Because you're the answer to everything in this life. It all begins by finally taking ownership of your life, the good and the bad, the tragedies, the highs and lows. It's all yours.

It has nothing to do with blame (blame is all about the past) but here's an easy way to tell the massive difference between blame and responsibility. Driving. You don't drive as if you're to blame, do you? You don't start the car up and immediately become defensive or feel racked with guilt or shame or regret as your foot pushes the accelerator and brings the beast to life. No, you drive your car, keeping the conditions in mind, being aware and doing everything that you need to do to ensure the completeness of your journey.

It's the same in life. Be responsible for your experience of how this is going.

At some point in this you might well start to see responsibility just the way I do.

As the greatest gift of your entire life.

You got the wheel baby, now drive this fucking thing.

"I don't love failure, but I'm not afraid of it either."

At least not afraid enough to stop.

There's this particularly annoying trend of people talking about how you must love failure, embrace failure; and some even profess to enjoy it!

Now, I'm not 100 percent against that as a kind of philosophy. I have no problem with fear of failure as a phenomenon. It's mostly healthy. At the very least, it gets you thinking about how you might currently deal with failure rather than avoiding it, but I'm not convinced by the notion of completely loving defeat. It's not only counterintuitive, it's also all too easily counterproductive.

So you'll need an empowering but realistic relationship with failure. Because in the end, if you're someone with any kind of bs busting success, it's unavoidable. You're going to suffer setbacks, from the minuscule to the colossal, on your path to whichever success you've tied your horse to. And even after you reach whatever it is you deem success to be, you're still not done with failure. Even the people on top of the mountain have to struggle with it.

So it makes sense to deal with failure and to put it in perspective. We work toward becoming comfortable with the *possibility* of failure. Not too comfortable, not in love with it, but just comfortable enough that you can see failure peeking out at you from the next horizon, but still you keep pushing. That it doesn't stop you dead in your tracks.

It's also about being able to fail without indulging yourself in all of the emotional baggage that comes with it. Not getting too discouraged, too depressed, or quitting too early when things go wrong. Failure is an intrinsic part of success. But there are also a load of people who've failed a million times and never succeeded. Who went through a dozen failed businesses or relationships without a single real success.

So rather than embracing failure directly, embrace the notion that it's not something you're willing to be stopped by. That it's all part of the game. What's your current relationship to failure?

This brings me to the drama of failure. As we talked about in the chapter about fear, we often build up realities in our minds about failure that aren't real. You're not going to die from your business going down the tubes or getting fired. You can take a breath, retool, and head off in another direction. You're alive—you have ideas and a pulse. That's a great start. Learn to be realistic about the implications of failure rather than worrying that you're going to die when it shows up.

"Being positive is overrated."

People love to talk about positivity. With a positive mind-set, we can achieve anything, we can change our lives, even change the world! BE POSITIVE!!

Hey, it's not like I hate positivity. It's not like I go around yelling at people that smile, telling the perennially upbeat how shit my day is, and occasionally pushing kindly old ladies over in the mall.

But the truth is, if you're out for financial or career or entrepreneurial or any other kind of success, there are going to come those times when you must produce, and yet every fiber of your being is screaming "NO!!!" Where you have heavy doubts or crippling confusion. Where you're resigned, depressed, or hopelessly cynical about the task ahead of you.

Some would say, "Well, you just gotta learn to be more positive!"

Don't bother, my friend. That's a detour you can't afford to get trapped in.

I'll admit to a certain satisfaction when I point to all the positive folks who thought they could do something—and failed. Those who were confident, inspired, even certain that they'd get it done—and didn't, even when blessed by a comforting blanket of positivity sparkle dust from head to toe. Why the satisfaction? I tend to see my mission to be a champion of the beaten down, of those who are overwhelmed and trapped, and simply to tell those people to be more positive is a horrific misunderstanding of what people are really dealing with.

Positivity is fine as a phenomenon, and hell, even a helpful tonic during the trek of turning your shit around, but that's about it as far as its usefulness in this life is concerned. I'm much more committed to people discovering that they can produce miraculous results regardless of how they feel rather than have them sidetracked by chasing the holy grail of positivity first.

Then there are those who are so freaking deeply encased in that fake shellac of positivity that even when they do fail spectacularly, they don't even realize or face the impact. Like the terrible singer who won't stop telling everyone about how they're going to be the next big thing or the desperate soul who watches their house burn down while being giggly grateful for the opportunity to warm their hands in the blazing inferno.

There's a bird called a starling that's attracted to shiny objects—silver, in particular. If you happen to come across one of their nests, you'll find all kinds of random scraps of metal, and maybe even a lost engagement ring or two.

Starlings are completely distracted with collecting these shiny things, just like the way we've become obsessed with the allure of being positive. It'll distract you from the mess of your nest or those hungry chicks of yours, but what the hell, though, there's a shiny Coke can ring pull, that'll look great in the collection. YAY!

And this is what the positivity obsession is: a distraction. While you're busily working toward a positive mind-set, there's shit all around you waiting to be done, but you'll either become sidetracked by your quest for some enthusiasm or motivation or, if you finally get it, become blinded by that sugary veil of positivity such that you might not see your little empire fracture and fall. Until it's too late.

One of those "came out of nowhere" results, right? No, you missed it entirely, even though it was right in front of your positive wee face.

There is only to do or not to do, and that's ultimately all you should be focusing on, whether it fills you with positivity or not. Because if you're honest with yourself, you'd realize there are countless things in your life that you've produced even while having an apparently negative mind-set. Hell, some of my life's greatest victories have come with the dull head-noise thud of "I can't do it" pulling me down every step of the way. I did it anyway.

You've done it too. You might've landed that job that you didn't think you would. You finished a project that, at various points, had you deeply doubting your own abilities. At the bottom end of the scale, you took out the trash or got out of bed when your motivation levels for those things were subterranean too. Positivity is fine. But it's just not a necessary component of being successful. I can understand, when you're fed a steady diet of positivity propaganda, the magnetic draw of all things sunny and shiny. Like all emotional states, positivity comes and goes, hangs around fleetingly or sometimes longer, but you should never use it as a sign of how or if you should proceed.

In fact, if there's anything you could start to develop, it would be the ability to act powerfully in your life in the absence of that positivity or motivation or enthusiasm.

Action is key; everything else is just noise.

"True strength doesn't come from your character, but from your willingness to go beyond it."

Who are you? No, really. Who *are* you?

Before you start waffling on about the spirit of the universe or something, let me tell you.

You're a bad actor.

Right now, you are little more than a series of predictable behaviors, thoughts, and emotions train-tracked into repeating neuronal patterns in your brain, and these "set ways" that you have become are all that you follow, day to day, scene to scene. It's your routine, your script, the archetype of your character.

For sure, you're always the lead in this little stage play of yours. Perhaps you're the mysterious yet charismatic rogue or the relentless comic who cries into their pillow or the broken angel fighting back against all the wrongdoings imposed upon you by this cruel and vicious world. Maybe you're the calming pragmatist, watching everyone else screwing up their world with more than a hint of arrogance in your eye and you're reading this book with your "I already know this" turned up to eleven in your head.

Every day, we look to that character for strength, we lean on it to get what we want. The comedian will use humor to bail them out of sticky situations or to have people like them. The pragmatist will study, take their time, and strategize their way through situation after situation, but here's the thing: if you want to accomplish new things in life, especially if they're big things, the kind of stuff you have never done before, that character isn't going to cut it. You'll need to find new ways to go beyond who you have come to know yourself as.

Success will come from getting off script, from breaking free from the constraints of who you've become. To take on new ways, to be courageous where you've previously backed off, to be patient where you've previously jumped in, and vice versa. You'll need to explore the full spectrum of "you" rather than rely on the narrow band of who you've become. You're a miracle of being, remember?

You could be anybody. Right now.

In this very moment you could be excited or inspired or powerful or passionate or courageous. Whichever "way of being" would allow you to step up and produce a new result in your life. The kind of beingness that breaks you free from the morass of your current character. You already have a deep and influential ability to bring yourself to life under any circumstance. It all just needs you to step up for yourself.

True strength isn't a product of character. True strength is when you're doing something you've never done before, when you're thinking "I don't know" or "I'm too tired" or "I can't do this" . . . and you go beyond.

Because that "beyond" is exactly where you'll find those new levels of strength and an array of wide-open pathways to new results for you to explore.

Again, if you're trying to get farther in life, to improve your future situation, to take it to the next level, you will have to face these tests of character. Times when the human being you have become is struggling to keep itself relevant. You might not be able to predict exactly what they'll be or when they'll pop up, but you can rest assured that they're coming.

At those moments, you have the choice to keep being that same character, or to change roles. To simply repeat your lines as they've been written—or to improvise, to ad-lib, to adjust to the challenges as they come and create new ways, new methods of overcoming them.

These are critical moments of reinvention, when you question all that you have become and step out into the unknown to explore who you could be, who you *need* to be, to break out of the familiar.

How do you do such a thing? You most likely already know the answer, although you've spent so long trying to talk yourself out of it that it's unreal to you.

That business, that job, that instrument, the paintbrush or sculpting clay or idea burning a hole in your conscious. Whether it's for love or passion or adventure or whatever, grab that possibility and embrace it as your own.

Step out here, into the unknown and unpredictable, and let the games begin.

"Life only ever changes in the paradigm of action."

You currently live in the crosshairs of two distinct worlds.

One is the internal world of thoughts, feelings, and emotions. The other is a world of behaviors, or in other words, actions. Now, of course, you think this is all just one world, which is a large part of why your life is the way it is. You spend large chunks of time trying to bring together these two separate and distinct worlds.

As a society, we've become increasingly obsessed with the idea of trying to make ourselves feel differently so that we can therefore do differently.

Change your thoughts/feelings/emotions, change your life, right? Wrong.

It's one of the dominant themes of most of the self-help shit out there these days too: seven steps to becoming more confident, boost your self-esteem in thirty days, increase your motivation with one simple daily trick. They're all vain attempts to somehow align your internal state with what's going on around you, and it seems like your life will be stuck until you get this shit in sync, right?

All of it revolves around creating a new emotional state. And from there, we're told, that new way of feeling will create the new ways of action we've always wanted. If only we just feel a little less depressed, more enthusiastic, we'll start taking the actions that lead us to where we want to go. We talked about this already when we looked at how positivity isn't the solution.

Here's why it doesn't work.

Because as human beings, all our successes—I'm talking 100 percent, every last one of them—came down to doing differently than we did before. The illusion is that sometimes it also included a change of how you felt, so you, like most people, made a false truth out of it. A bad wisdom.

Sure, sometimes changing the way we feel smooths the motivation to change what we do, but changing what we do is what makes the change happen in reality, in the physical world. Doing in the absence of the feeling of motivation or confidence or whatever, still works. New feelings without action change nothing. As an added bonus, changing our actions even changes how we feel along the way too.

It's why you feel more motivated and happier to work out *after* you've started working out, not before.

Now, I know I'm going against the grain a little here, but if you're not taking consistent action to further your future, then everything else is just imaginary bs.

Everything worthwhile—in our lives and in history—started with a small action. That's why I'm telling you to bring all of your attention, all of your brain and energy to impacting the world of action. To begin to build a life centered around increasing and changing your actions, not shifting emotions.

There's nothing wrong with improving your mood or your confidence, but the surer path to success is when you do things differently, even when you feel the same. When you feel like shit but still knock out that project. When you're feeling anxious or even scared but still ask that person out. When you're feeling distracted but you study anyway.

In most professions, you don't get paid less if you do your job while you're in some negative mood as long as you do your job. But you do get paid less (read: nothing) if you don't do the work while you're floating on cloud nine.

That's because it's the action that matters, not how you feel.

Kinda brings a whole new meaning to the phrase "get your act together" now, doesn't it?

11

A Wise as #@%! Life

We're out for a
life that matters.
A life of purpose.
A Wise as Fu*k life.

It's almost time for us to part ways, and I want to leave you with something truly life-altering.

I've packed as much wisdom into these pages as I could without turning it into a monster that no one would have any time to read. These days, it seems we are being front-loaded, back-loaded, and generally just overloaded with information and demands on our time.

But we've covered some important ground. It's now on you to start taking on some of these fundamental parts of life and really think through and deal with what needs to guide you. What incorrect assumptions have you been making above love that it's time to scrap? What have you let derail you when it comes to fear or loss or success? It really is up to you to stake your claim for the life you want, one based on something more tangible than your seesaw of everyday emotions and stories that have thus far ruled the roost of your thoughts and responses.

When you feel like you have a grasp on those fundamentals, I would like you to take a moment with me to ponder your life's work.

Yes, that's right, your life's work. Your masterpiece, your opus, the blinding glory of your existence.

You know, the thing that will remain here after you're gone. Your influence, your legacy. Now, I don't care if you're twenty or eighty, this is a question everyone needs to face right now. Haven't you ever at least pondered what you are leaving in your wake? What are you out to leave behind?

I remember when I was fifteen or sixteen years old, talking with my best mate (he's still my best mate too by the way), wondering about our futures. He asked me, "What do you want to do?"

I responded, "I don't know, but I want it to be something that lives on after I die."

Now, it would be so powerful and magical if I were to tell you how that statement burned a life-altering purpose into my heart and drove me to become the man I am today but . . . it didn't. I let it waft from my lips and into that Scottish summer sky, only for it to be eagerly consumed by the idling, trifling conversation that followed. Something about music and soccer.

Turns out I wasn't too good at those things either.

I went on to wrestle with my life for the first forty years of it, and I was mostly losing.

I lived an ordinary, unremarkable life, and not just because I am ordinary (I am, and we all are) but also because I wasn't up to anything that would force me to rise out of the mud. Basically, my life wasn't being used for anything other than the humdrum concerns of the given day, week, or month.

Earn money, make friends, find a partner, buy a house, go on vacations, complain, have fun, complain, have more fun, complain again, pay the bills, try to get ahead, pursue a dream or two, more vacations, pay more bills, more house, more car, try to get along with my family—you get the picture. I mean, it's what everyone else was doing, so why not?

It's probably a lot like yours too.

I never really woke up until I was forty. Until then I was locked in my head and pursuing what seemed "realistic" from the confines of my own homespun little jam jar.

If I had kept going, I'm absolutely positive my later years would have held nothing but regret.

Sure, I had my successes, sure, I had friends and family and a roof over my head, but they didn't mean my life was heading anywhere near the longed-for land of satisfaction and happiness. And if you step back and start to cut to the chase with yourself, it's completely fine to have all of these things be part of your life, but it still does not address what your life is being used for.

I had a "doing" life, just like you, and I needed a "being" life, just like you too. I was in dire need of a life that called me to *be* someone I had never been before and that demanded I rise to it each and every day. A life that forced me to respond, and I had to put that shit together myself.

There came a point for me when I had to ask myself, "If I keep doing this, how does it all turn out for me?" The answer screamed back at me from the abyss of my future. It doesn't turn out. I die struggling and hoping and trying, perhaps sedated by a hopeful optimism or philosophical shrug. Here's the deal: how do you answer that question for yourself? Take away the hope and tell the truth.

Think about this for a moment. Look at the trajectory of your life, all the things you are currently putting up with or putting off, suffering under or struggling with. Follow that spiral all the way down in your mind's eye. Your relationships, your body, your finances, your passions, your triggers and afflictions, and your affinity for that burdensome past of yours. Get connected to your reality, the weight of everything you have going on. This isn't a theory or a dress rehearsal for some later life; this is it, this is your life.

How does this turn out for you if you keep living the way you do?

I'll wait a while as you let the answer sink in.

Picture it right now, the stone-cold, harsh reality of what's to come along this particular pathway.

See it? Okay. Breathe. Exhale. Push the air out of your lungs.

This doesn't have to be you. You can change. Today. I don't care how old you are, how screwed you think you are, or how trapped you've become. I'm going to show you how to live a real, workable, life-on-track, steady-as-she-goes, Wise as Fu*k life.

IT'S NOT ABOUT YOU AND
IT NEVER HAS BEEN

Putting it bluntly, we desire freedom. And more specifically, freedom of self. Which, by default, requires you to become increasingly obsessed, with self and with all that differentiates you from everyone else. It's little wonder we have become so fascinated with ourselves.

But why not, right? I mean, we have dreams and ambitions and rights and . . . hold on there, my freedom-loving friend, I need you to consider the wider picture too.

You see, we're also now ocean-deep into the "what about me?" generation, or rather, series of generations, and not only is it big business, but also business is good! Everything around you is about you, for you, aimed at you, serving you, demanding your attention and feeding your ravenous need for self.

The problem is, the more it's about you, the more fucked *we* are. No, really. That's not only true about your most intimate relationships, it's also true about your relationships with the world itself.

Think about yourself for a moment here (like you need an invitation for such a thing), when someone has something you don't and you immediately start to ponder, *What about me?* We see someone's relationship and compare our state of bliss—or who's keeping us from it. Then there are those times when we see someone else's expression, their freedom to be, as an infringement on our own. We look out and look in, out and in, comparing and contrasting over and over, caught in a trap of not enough/never enough.

I'm going to use a word here that I don't like to use.

Narcissist.

Why don't I like to use it? Because people use that word to label and write *others* off. It eventually allows the user to categorize someone. To turn them into a "thing" with certain properties rather than a living, breathing being with wants and needs and a past of their own to overcome. At some level we're all struggling, no matter how it looks on the surface. Keep that in mind.

The one place where it's okay to use that word is with oneself. To examine, to take stock, and to take some ownership of where we are drifting. To reveal the narcissist within.

Be honest, you're fascinated with yourself. It's why you bought this book.

You could also argue that it's not just you and that it's been like this for a long time, though it's maybe a little more obvious these days, with the world of social media, reality TV, selfies, and everything else ramming it in our face 24/7. But try on the idea that "the world" is only ever responding to you, and yes, you're that powerful.

Let's dive into this a little here.

The past few hundred years have been one big, prolonged revolution. And yes, we're still in the middle of it right now. But I'm not talking so much about the obvious and famous physical revolutions, when people took up arms, filled the streets, fighting or protesting a monarch or a government or injustice or a way of life. Sure, there have been plenty of those throughout history and there most likely always will be in some version or another, but in my mind these are all simply a product of what has really been taking place. As an example, the emergence of the United

States was a prime example of a systemic and colossal change that was (and still is) sweeping across the planet.

But what is it that has been changing so dramatically and powerfully?

Our thinking and, by default, our talking. The evolution of humanity is a conversational one. We are using language to forge new freedoms, new ideas, new permissions to express and create who we are in language, and this change has been charging like a tsunami toward the future and clearing a new pathway for generations to come.

There is a long and storied history of human beings reaching for something better, to improve life and embrace new levels of freedom, rightfully so, but like every solution, no matter how justified or right, it comes with certain consequences. The kind of results we might not have seen coming but nonetheless eventually cost us something.

Of course, we want the obvious freedoms of choosing who we vote for or what group we're a part of, what social or financial class we belong to, where we live and in what kind of home we live in.

And all of that is built on your greatest desire. Your desire to fundamentally choose who you are and who you could be. Your self-expression. Your expression of self.

Now, of course, all of that is a lot more possible these days, and I'm certainly not saying anything is inherently wrong with that desire to choose what you think or how you act. Far from it.

But try on the idea that this quest for freedom has also come at a significant cost, the kind of cost that is mostly hidden and continues to grow and embolden in the background of not only your life but also all of our lives.

What cost? Haven't you noticed we're becoming more and more insular, more internal and inward-facing, more anxious, more worried, more concerned, and all the while developing a greater and deeper separation from the people and world around us?

That's the cost of the freedom to be ourselves that we've demanded. We've become trapped in self-examination and absorption, burdened by what we think we deserve, and driven by our deepest, most inauthentic wants.

But since you're not perfect (even after all that examining), this actually turns into a mindless fascination endlessly picking fluff out of your own belly button. You become obsessed with your weaknesses or failures, with what you think you're lacking or need. You relive those embarrassing or traumatizing moments from your past again and again by continually trying to get over, get past, or ignore them. Scratch that goddamn itch and plug that freaking hole.

There's so little external reflection, a clear view of what's going on in the world, that the brunt of your attention turns inward, where it finds and focuses on every single thing you don't like or are uncomfortable with.

And thus, rather than some newfound ability to be who you want to be, you actually become more worried and more anxious with what you are not. And so the cycle goes. You feel anxiety or resignation over your weight or your appearance, your career or finances, your character flaws and failings. The worry that everyone is getting ahead while you're standing still. The phobia of being left behind.

And all this internalization has also caused us to drift away from something that we're really good at and flourish with: connection.

THE TRIBE

By nature, we're tribal. Even your silent singularity or desire for independence is only ever in contrast to the group. By and large we prefer to congregate in packs, whether it's a family unit, friend group, a village, a town, or a city. And that "group," in many ways, should be bigger and more connected than ever before, due to bigger populations, easier travel, and the advances of technology that we have accepted into our everyday lives.

Yet we *feel* totally disconnected. We're actually using these advances to hide behind online personas while passively (and sometimes overtly) aggressively voicing our upsets, concerns, fears, and differences anonymously. The apparent trauma of eye contact and face-to-face conversation is growing by the day.

If you lived five hundred years ago, you would have been part of something that felt real and tangible (although unseen), and your prominence in any group would have been related to whatever you were providing for the whole. There was nowhere to hide. Whether you were the seamstress, the hunter, or the medicine man, the farmer, locksmith, maid, or the local baker, you were a participant, someone who was there to play a specific role in the group. And for you to be successful then, you'd have to get out of your head and into your life. Where was that life? Back then, as it is now, your life and the quality of your life was weaved in conversation and relationship with others.

In very simple terms you found yourself consumed by the life you were weaving with other people. And it was an activity, not a pursuit.

Maybe it was big, maybe it was small, but you knew what was needed from you, and you provided it. This made you important to the group, critical to its function, even if it was digging graves or sweeping chimneys or making yarn. But it wasn't just the task, it was who the task demanded you *be* in that group. Read that again. And yes, it wasn't a fairy-tale existence, either. But I'll get to that; just stick with me here.

Now there's no longer a demand on you to rise, to show up as someone in this life anymore. So in you go, exploring the darkness and shadows of your own little world, and that's who you've become. Trying to spin yourself a thick coat of positivity, internal instead of external.

Lost in the maze of your feelings and pains.

Your life right now, when seen through this lens of conversation, makes total sense. It's not what you're up against that has you by the throat but rather what you say about what you're up against that's fucking you over and, as I've said in my other books, your emotions and your talk are dance partners.

Therefore you're not a creature of feelings and thoughts. You, my linguistic little friend, are a creature of language, and every moment of every day you are creating your experience of being alive with every word, phrase, and complaint. And not just your own experience. People have ears, remember? You have influence. That's right, you; but you're so blind to it, so dumbed down by your own self-interest and what you're lacking, you can't see the power you already have.

I'm not saying you should return to medieval or precolonial life, so you can loosen the death grip you have on your cellphone. There was a helluva lot wrong with society then too. People lived in poverty and degradation. They were exposed to systemic bigotry, misogyny, racism, inhumanity, and cruelty at levels that are hard to comprehend when compared to most modern societies today. It's not hard to see why that spark of self-interest became such a burning sea of fire when you look at those items.

But I'm also inviting you to consider that in this process of gaining freedom we are losing something that's critically important to our own humanity.

Us. That you are in fact a "we."

We're losing the idea of the group, and no, I don't mean the industrially trimmed down, sterilized, and acceptable-to-you team of agreeable robots you surround yourself with here either. I mean ALL of us, the entire group. And we're losing who we are in it.

Now, what do we provide? As a society we're obsessed with consumption, with getting what we need, and it's not just material things. We want joy, love, accomplishment, recognition, admiration, or connection, but haven't you ever noticed how everyone is seeking these things?

For instance, look at the rise of "online influencers." You might cast a cynical eye in their direction and arrogantly wonder what the big deal is with those folks. You could perhaps follow their words or ideas or advice for some kind of respite in your life. But this phenomenon can only exist because so many people are *seeking* influence, and when I say "people," I mean you. We live in a world of emotional vampires, and if you're thinking of others when I use this term, you're missing the point and the opportunity. Keep this in house for once.

The march of "What about me?" is devouring everything in its path, and few are paying attention because the shiny allure of personal freedom or self-expression or future success has hypnotized the masses.

Where have all the contributors gone? No one is standing for anything.

Sure, there are some, but the world is filled with the unfulfilled, the broken, the lost, and the angry. Everyone is looking for an answer, but few are giving their lives to *being* an answer in this life.

Now, as usual, I have to add a little caveat here for my committed victims. Because there are people who are going to read this and say, "But Gary, I'm always putting others before myself, and I'm not thriving."

Try this on. You might do things with the notion that you're helping others for the sake of helping them, but what if that's yet another strategy of yours to "get" something, and the only reason it's so draining is because it never quite gets you the thing you're *really* after? You see, if it's not empowering you, that's usually a sign that you're being driven by some hidden want or need regardless of what you tell yourself. Whether it's a physical reward, some feel-good emotion such as admiration or pride, or even some sense of superiority or absolution from your past, you're after something other than what's on the surface.

In other words, it's not authentic, it's not genuine. It's what I call a "strategic" contribution. You take out the trash, but it's only so you can earn "points" with your partner for future use. Strategy. You volunteer at some nonprofit, but that's so you can convince yourself you really are better than your guilt or shame or some other of your darkest thoughts. Strategy. You are kind and compassionate with people, but really you want to make sure they don't become confrontational, so you use your amenable ways to manipulate them into shape. Strategy. You help your kid with their homework because you want them to be successful—but it's actually so you can look good to others. Strategy.

It's all trying to make up for something, and no matter your "contribution" you'll notice the same thing. It's always ultimately about YOU. Even if you don't see it or are initially struggling to come to terms with it here.

"But, Mr. Scottish person, surely it's good to do some of these things even if they are strategic?!!"

Look, it's generally a good thing to do a good thing in this world, every little bit helps, but this is about you finally living a Wise as Fu*k life, the kind of life that fulfills you. But you'll never get what you want if you keep tagging your strategies onto your good deeds.

It's not only inauthentic and burdensome, but it's sneaky too! You're playing games with people that they can't see (although like you, they probably have their suspicions), you're going around doing one thing while meaning another thing entirely, and your upsets arise when the people in your life don't respond to your hidden strategies. Then the resentment kicks in . . .

There are always things you'll need to give up, a skin to shed as you re-create your life, and this is most certainly one of those items. Let go of your more obvious strategies of manipulation (yes, that's what it is) and look for the more subterranean ones, the kind of internal programming that you've lumped yourself with that only complicates your life.

Deal with your fears, your concerns and hopes, live your life out here in the open. You won't always get what you want, but your mind will be clear and your baggage light as you prepare yourself for what's next and what's next and what's next.

The pathway to freedom is initially shocking (as you first confront what you now need to do), bumpy and messy (as you start to take care of those things), and finally easy and graceful as you begin taking on life in a new clearing of authenticity and power.

We're out for a life that matters. A life of purpose. A Wise as Fu*k life.

12

The Contributing Factor

Wake yourself up to what's important, to what actually matters in this life. Set aside your fears and failures, stop obsessing over gaining success or avoiding pain, and finally show up as the kind of human being you have always wanted to be. Not only to make a difference but to **be** *that difference so that all people are impacted.*

Human beings are hardwired to connect and make a difference with each other, and yes, that includes you too.

In our society most of us are racing toward riches or recognition or admiration, but if you took a moment to see what people do *after* they fulfill those kinds of dreams you'd start to understand what drives us authentically as human beings. To what actually fulfills and nurtures and connects us.

Look at what people do when they've finally accomplished what they thought was their heart's desire, when they eventually get to the end of their personal rainbow. When the mountains of money and awards stopped meaning anything, those people naturally turned back toward their authentic expression. People such as Steve Jobs, Bill Gates, all the way back to John D. Rockefeller, returned to their humanity and their deep-seated need to genuinely contribute. Their lives became about making a difference for others with no intention other than to make that difference. It's that selfless contribution that truly makes for a Wise as Fu*k life. That's the secret. All of it.

But what difference are you making?

None.

Don't get offended here; get interested, get your eyes off the mirage of survival and "making it" for a minute, set aside your resignation, reasons, and excuses, and jump in with me.

Here's some cold truth. You don't consciously influence life itself. You don't contribute. You're so wrapped up in your own little bit of real estate, you're missing the point of being alive.

Like everyone else, you're in servitude to yourself, in permanent service to your own self-indulgence and self-made rat race. You're a seesaw of predictable emotions and feelings with no real sense of your power to rise to something far greater. Why? Well, it's not about selfishness, even though that's what it produces.

You've completely bought into the notion that there's somewhere you need to get to, a future when this shit all turns out for you, and that you'll need to bite, kick, and scream your way there. But most importantly, you relate to yourself as an impostor, and therefore, in a very deep and profound way, you don't think you *can* make a difference. You're too small, too powerless, not skilled enough, not smart enough, don't have the reputation or charisma or whatever to be a force of nature in this life of yours. After all, you're just one in almost eight billion people, right? A face among the masses, a wispy dot in a vast universe of endless dots, so you've resigned yourself to playing this tiny, insignificant, and pointless game.

The game of you.

And then you wonder why you're never quite happy or satisfied or fulfilled.

It then stands to reason that if you can't make that kind of difference, if you cannot create and impact life, you, like everyone else, must fundamentally relate to yourself like you're without power, like you just don't *matter* in the big picture. That's right, you think you don't matter.

Let that sink in for a moment.

Take as long as you like.

That's everything right there. That's the short, cut-the-shit answer to why you live like you do.

Follow the tracks here and this is what you'll find. Regardless of what you might say or even think, you *live* like you don't matter. Somewhere, underneath the layers of emotion, memory, and automatic response, we feel it's not good enough, that it won't make a difference, that we're ultimately not needed beyond the limits of our own lives. Why bother going through the trouble if no one will notice or ever really appreciate it?

Even worse, maybe they'll just laugh at you or treat you with derision over your attempts to make a difference. Defining yourself by the reactions of others again, huh?

Deep down, you're coming at life from a place of "I don't matter." That's a completely treasonous act, a profound and wounding betrayal of self at your own hand. And all your striving in this life is about trying to prove that you somehow do or eventually will someday.

You, my remarkable force of nature, have become small, petty, and insignificant, dulled by you to keep you safe, coddled . . . and small. The world didn't do this to you, it wasn't your mom or your issues, or your ex or your story, it was *you*, and you did it systematically and clinically. You've written yourself off.

You might already have been arguing your logic these past few pages. Making your case about the struggles of paying your bills or losing that weight, or getting that job, business, or degree going. Maybe you just need that jolt of confidence or to let your past go or get over that trauma. Perhaps you already know you have no voice beyond your immediate circle or are lacking in the expertise or know-how. I know, I know, you're not a billionaire either, you don't have those kinds or resources. Right?

Not everyone can be Bill Gates anyway, so you just need me to help little old you get your shit together and *then* you'll make a difference for others. But just STOP!

That's what *everyone* is already doing. Gimme, gimme, gimme!

Can't you see that this is the logic of the vampire?

"But I do contribute!"

The illusion is that you, like everyone else, think you're contributing by giving your time or your money or your skill. "Oh, yes, I like to give back" as you sign your fifty-dollar check to save the kitty cats or spend your annual two hours at the local soup kitchen. Ugh. That's not *being* a contribution, that's *making* a contribution. That's not the kind of contribution that makes for a Wise as Fu*k life! There's nothing wrong with making a contribution—it helps in little ways, sometimes big ways—but it will never make up for the life-inducing, awe-inspiring magnitude of giving your life to *being* a contribution.

I'm not saying any of this from a pedestal. I'm not guilting or shaming or whatevering you here. That's an easy card to pull whenever human beings are confronted by what they don't like or agree with. You are reading this book so you can get an access to a great life, right? Good. I'm talking to the right person then. This is it; this is what it takes to live a fulfilled and happy life, and there's no escaping it.

No amount of money or accolades (no matter how much you want to give it a try) will ever substitute the richness of actually being someone who impacts and influences, someone who lives their life as a demonstration of what's possible. It's not just influencing but rather "being" that influence. It's not about being perfect, either. It's all about participating in this game, the game of contribution. You'll fail and win, you'll get caught up in the spider's web of your own survival and then awaken to something greater, and you'll do this time and again, over and over, day upon day.

Does that mean you have to give up your goal of that Bugatti or that business or that book or relationship? NO! You can still have all those things to aim for, but when you start organizing your life around what matters, you'll have a life that matters, one that fills your cup and recognizes who you are.

A LIFE BIGGER THAN YOURSELF

This is what it takes to live a Wise as Fu*k life, to every day get your nose out of your basest needs, wants, or desires, to set aside your fears and failures, to stop obsessing over gaining success or avoiding pain, and to get out there into the world and finally show up as the kind of human being you have always wanted to be. To bring yourself fully to every conversation, every interaction with the idea that you're there to not only make a difference but to *be* that difference so that all people are impacted.

So what's the alternative to this ordinary, self-serving, humdrum bullshit that you've made your life about?

How about you become a player? Someone who gets themselves on the hook for how life is going and, no, not just your own. Someone who gives a fuck about their environment and is out to influence. An influencer.

But Gary, didn't you just say influencers are usually full of bs? Here's the thing. To be a real-life influencer, someone who brings life to life, you simply need to change your freaking talk!

You don't need more money or knowledge or experience or time to be that person. You don't need a steady flow of Oprah-quality life-giving advice or a dazzling Instagram account with a million followers or Pixar-quality memes on your Facebook feed with a PhD in philosophy to back it up, either.

Look around you. Instead of complaining or gossiping about the people you share your life with, how are they doing? Your partner, your family, friends, workmates, your ex or that old schoolmate, your neighbors, the barista at Starbucks who makes your coffee every day, the Uber driver or the customer service person who answers when you're calling about your fucked-up credit card bill.

Who are *you* for these people? Are you someone who confirms their resignation or cynicism in those petty day-to-day meanderings of bullshit, or are you out to make a difference in their world? What's your contribution? How are you showing up?

What do you bring to the table in this life?

If your first answer is about some excuse or explanation or justification for what you do, you're a poster child for what I'm talking about! The secret to a life of fulfillment, accomplishment, and happiness is to make your life about *who you are for others*, not to spend your life gorging yourself on an aimless attempt to fill the black hole that currently rests in the pit of your gut or soul or chakra or wherever and then find a little group where you can complain about your struggles over a glass (or ten) of wine, by the end of which everybody's a little happier (or at least tipsier) but no one has changed.

I'm well aware of the glut of posts, memes, and videos on social media telling us to "Be kind" or "Have compassion," but the reality is we mostly think we *are* kind or compassionate or accepting or loving, etc., but this is your chance to tell yourself the truth. How many times do you go into the day with "kindness" or "understanding" on your mind? How many times do you deliberately bring a conscious and purposeful self to bear in your life? Even when you do, think of the times you've all too easily sold out on that because of what someone else did or didn't do or some random event that crossed your path and doused your fire.

No matter your answer to this, the good news is that you can do it today. Take three honest and deliberate actions to be kind. Or loving. Or patient. Or understanding. Or vulnerable. Choose something, live a deliberate life. Intervene. Contribute. Then choose something else and go with that.

It takes effort to be someone in this life. You don't get to be considered unique or extraordinary by floating along as your already determined default self, trying to come up with smart ideas or strategies for your own success while occasionally glancing back at the good bits to fool yourself with your heavily edited, easy-to-swallow past.

It's easy to be liked by some people. Sure, flashing a pile of hundred-dollar bills hanging off the end of your pirate-themed silver-ring fingers or having your arse squeezed into those industrial-strength spandex yoga pants might get you likes on Instagram, but it won't get you fulfillment, peace of mind, or the magic of being your greatest you.

I can hear the excuses coming. You have problems? So does everyone. It's called being alive. You'll always have one problem or another or fifty. If you measure your life by how you're doing getting rid of your problems, you'll never be happy because there's always another one just waiting to happen.

You can have problems and be happy; it's not either/or.

An extraordinary, vibrant, and captivating life is available to you, but you need to stop the lunacy of looking for it. You *are* it, Sherlock! It's all in how you be and act, and you don't need anything fancy to transform that shit.

What you *do* need is to wake yourself up to what's important, to what actually matters in this life. YOU matter, YOU make a difference, YOU already have the ability to influence and create life in your speaking and in your very being. And until that becomes an intentional, conscious, and deliberate way of living, you're on autopilot with the rest of the drones.

You're not a person, you're a phenomenon, and all it takes to unleash this phenomenon is for you to stand for a possibility in the face of the cynicism, to be adventurous in the presence of fear, to be accepting or forgiving or loving when presented with anger or resentment, to be compassionate when every bone in your body screams to defend yourself.

"But Gary, how do I do that?"

You take a leap, the kind of leap that someone who is committed to adventure or acceptance or love or whatever would take in their life. If you're committed to love, for instance, what is an action you could take right now that's aligned with that commitment? What do you need to say, and to whom?

Do it! Right now!

What if you don't get the response you were looking for? So what?! Be the phenomenon you are regardless of outcomes. Then you really are a breathing, thriving, relentless force of nature.

Using this book to impact your life will require you to take a transformed view, to be open to the idea of being truly unique, of taking the right road instead of the easy or typical one, and to be true to what you believe rather than bending, shaping, or breaking yourself up to be liked or accepted or to fit in. To be yourself.

You devote yourself to being bigger than the life you used to have. To be the source of life itself rather than yet another boring and insipid commentator, observer, and/or justified victim, looking at life from twenty thousand feet and complaining at what you're seeing from there.

IT'S SHOWTIME

There's a reason why I peacefully and gracefully don't give a fuck about what others think of me. It's simple. It's not like I'm a robot without feelings or fears or triggers like everyone else, it's just that I'm gripped by something else entirely. I'm engrossed in the game, not the spectators. I put myself, my thoughts, my ideas, and my passion into this game. I'm not angry at the observers; I expect them. They ultimately have no impact on me, because if they did, that would be about me. My life isn't about me, it's about you and how I might be of service to life. That's THE game!

I live my life in service of others. I'm not being noble or generous or enlightened FFS, I'm simply committed to a great life. And that's the one surefire way that I know how to have one.

"Yeah, that's all very fine and good for someone like you, Gary, but my life is different, there are so many bullshitters and shysters and people out to get for themselves."

I'm well aware of that. Have there been people who have tried to or actually taken advantage of how I live my life? Well, I'd hope so! I'm out to be a presence in the world, not to hide in a cupboard! However, I could count the number of times I've been fucked over in this life on one hand. Why? I'm not giving my attention or energy to that shit. There might have been a lot of occasions—who knows? But all my effort, all my focus is on what's possible. All the time, every time. I'm much more fascinated by what's next than by what has been, and you should be too.

I'm aware, I'm responsible, but most of all, I'm all-the-fuck in.

If you join in this game, the game of influencing all that is going on around you, I have all the respect in the world for you. For those who spend their lives in pious, disconnected judgment of it? I pass. I move on. I don't have time for that shit.

Why should you join the game? BECAUSE YOU FUCKING CAN! This is available to you right now and right now and right now.

In this very moment you can be the kind of human being who shifts people just by entering the room rather than by your reputation or your dress sense, bogus charisma, or pearly-white teeth. By showing up as someone worth aspiring to. Not boastful or arrogant or flashy but by being the kind of human others can find respite in or even aspire to be.

Be the fucking change you wish to see, for the love of God! If love is missing? Be that. If connection is absent? Be that. If it's understanding, friendship, or acceptance that's needed, it's time for you to show up big, and all without turning it into a strategy for something in return. No judgment, no excuses, no blaming; show up.

The less you make your life about you, the better you'll do. I know that sounds counterintuitive. I know some might be so tightly wound around the idea of survival, they are terrified of letting go, but that's the straight of it. Be bigger than your concerns, greater than your worries or anxieties. And how you do that is by starting to get your attention on your influence. On your *total* impact.

Being a contribution requires no skill, no resources, no drummed-up fake-ass emotional state to get you on the map. This about you finally realizing your power, your innate talent for consciously shifting the direction of life itself.

Someone a lot smarter than I once told me "I can't pee for you," and that statement is true for you too.

I can't make you do this, I can't wean you off your addiction to self, your problems, and your fascination for daydreaming your life away and wasting these precious moments of your existence in self-pity and the pointless search for something you already are.

The clock is ticking. You have less time today than you had yesterday, and it will be the same tomorrow.

Tick fucking tock.

Join me, come down here, into the game, make a difference, play it fast and hard, and give it everything you've got. Then get up tomorrow and do it again. Then again. And again. And you can do it all while you're setting goals, building an empire, getting in shape, fixing your finances, starting your business; it really doesn't matter because who you are screams your passion for life.

This is not about waiting until your shit's together before casting your eyes out into the world; you can do both, and in a way that invigorates and enlivens you.

History only remembers the players, not who had the best seats, and while a lot of people already know that, they have bought into the idea of someday *becoming* a player rather than grabbing the opportunity of getting in the game right now.

This is your shot—it's now, today, there is no later. Be a player.

About the Author

Born and raised in Glasgow, Scotland, Gary John Bishop moved to the United States in 1997. This opened up his pathway to the world of personal development, specifically to his love of ontology and phenomenology. This approach, in which he trained for a number of years, saw him rise to become a senior program director with one of the world's leading personal development companies. After years of facilitating programs for thousands of people all over the world and later studying and being influenced by the philosophies of Martin Heidegger, Hans-Georg Gadamer, and Edmund Husserl, Gary is producing his own brand of "urban philosophy." His lifelong commitment to shifting people's ability to exert real change in their lives drives him each and every day. He has a no-frills, no-bullshit approach that has brought him an ever-increasing following, drawn to the simplicity and real-world use of his work.

A few more words of wisdom . . .

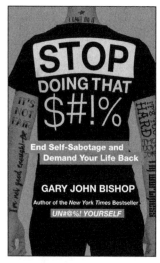

Available wherever books, ebooks, and audiobooks are sold.